"The Object Lessons series achieves close to magic: the books take ordinary—even banal—objects and animate them with a rich history of invention, political struggle, science, and popular mythology. Filled with fascinating details and conveyed in sharp, accessible prose, the books make the everyday world come to life. Be warned: once you've read a few of these, you'll start walking around your house, picking up random objects, and musing aloud: 'I wonder what the story is behind this thing?'"

Steven Johnson, author of *Where Good Ideas Come From* and *How We Got to Now*

"In 1957 the French critic and semiotician Roland Barthes published *Mythologies*, a groundbreaking series of essays in which he analysed the popular culture of his day, from laundry detergent to the face of Greta Garbo, professional wrestling to the Citroën DS. This series of short books, Object Lessons, continues the tradition."

Melissa Harrison, *Financial Times*

"Though short, at roughly 25,000 words apiece, these books are anything but slight."

Marina Benjamin, *New Statesman*

OBJECTLESSONS

A book series about the hidden lives of ordinary things.

Series Editors:

Ian Bogost and Christopher Schaberg

Advisory Board:

Sara Ahmed, Jane Bennett, Jeffrey Jerome Cohen,
Johanna Drucker, Raiford Guins, Graham Harman,
renée hoogland, Pam Houston, Eileen Joy, Douglas
Kahn, Daniel Miller, Esther Milne, Timothy Morton,
Kathleen Stewart, Nigel Thrift, Rob Walker, Michele White.

In association with

Georgia Center for
Tech Media Studies

BOOKS IN THE SERIES

egg

NICOLE WALKER

Bloomsbury Academic
An imprint of Bloomsbury Publishing Inc

B L O O M S B U R Y
NEW YORK • LONDON • OXFORD • NEW DELHI • SYDNEY

Bloomsbury Academic

An imprint of Bloomsbury Publishing Inc

1385 Broadway
New York
NY 10018
USA

50 Bedford Square
London
WC1B 3DP
UK

www.bloomsbury.com

**BLOOMSBURY and the Diana logo are trademarks of Bloomsbury
Publishing Plc**

First published 2017

Library of Congress Cataloging-in-Publication Data
Names: Walker, Nicole.
Title: Egg / Nicole Walker.
Description: New York, NY, USA : Bloomsbury Academic, an imprint of
Bloomsbury Publishing Inc., 2017. | Series: Object lessons | Includes
bibliographical references and index.
Identifiers: LCCN 2016031062 (print) | LCCN 2016037323 (ebook) | ISBN
9781501322853 (pbk. : alk. paper) | ISBN 9781501322860 (ePub) | ISBN
9781501322877 (ePDF)
Subjects: LCSH: Eggs–Philosophy–Popular works. | Eggs–Social
aspects–Popular works. | Cooking (Eggs)–Popular works.
Classification: LCC TX745 .W28 2017 (print) | LCC TX745 (ebook) | DDC
641.6/75–dc23
LC record available at https://lccn.loc.gov/2016031062

ISBN: PB: 978-1-5013-2285-3
ePub: 978-1-5013-2286-0
ePDF: 978-1-5013-2287-7

Series: Object Lessons

Cover design: Alice Marwick

Typeset by Deanta Global Publishing Services, Chennai, India
Printed and bound in the United States of America

For Rebecca and for Egg

CONTENTS

ACKNOWLEDGMENTS

I want to thank the kind, generous people who told me their egg stories. Thank you, my dear friends, Tanya Wojtowych, Margot Singer, Okim Kang, and the scholars who traveled to Northern Arizona University from China to study here, Wiehong Wang, Hui Lang, Hailing Lu. Thank you, Angie Hansen, for helping me connect with the Chinese scholars and for your belief in this book. Thank you, Karen Renner, for your smart suggestions and thank you Anita Singh for your thorough and supportive notes throughout the copy editing process. Thank you Haaris Naqvi and Ian Bogost for your support of EGG and your work on the entire Object Lessons series. Thank you in particular to editor Christopher Schaberg who championed EGG from the get-go. Thank you, Julie Paegle, for reading every manuscript and making it better. Thank you Eleanor and Rick Spearman for making time for me to write by taking the kids fun places. Thank you especially to Rebecca Campbell for inspiring me for the past 30 years. I am lucky to call you my friend. And thank you, Erik, for being a good egg, and thanks, Max and Zoe, for sharing your mom with her typing machine.

"Spoons" published in the *Los Angeles Review of Books*, Spring 2015.

"Mohawk" and "Rotten Eggs" forthcoming in *forty fifth Parallel*, Spring 2016.

Dear egg,

It is possible that humanity is built on the many proteins of your baby-chick deferred, extruded product of bird. You, egg, may be the amalgam that holds the planet together. You come from everywhere. From egg drop soup in China to avgolemono in Greece, from omelets in France to Nigerian egg roll, you are the gluey common denominator among the variable spices.

You hold together cakes, both pan and chocolate. You lift up soufflés and harden meringues. You are the hard-boiled defense against hunger carried to work via purse, lunch box, airplane tote. In times of plenty, we roll you down the hill and let you crack for the seagulls. In times of scarcity, we tuck you in piles of salt and pray you last until winter.

When my daughter, Zoe, was in the hospital with respiratory syncytial virus (RSV), my husband Erik and I forgot to eat. We watched as the respiratory therapist pounded her back to shake the congestion from her lungs; we watched as nurses suctioned fluid with tubes through her nostrils. We stood by and watched because there wasn't much else we could do. To keep our strength up, my husband rode home on his skateboard to gather lunch. He invariably came back with eggs, hard-boiled. We peeled the eggs and watched Zoe breathe. We sliced the eggs. We watched Zoe breathe. We shook salt and pepper on our eggs and we watched Zoe breathe and breathe until they took the supplemental oxygen away.

When we were finally able to bring her home, it was an explosion of egg. No more hard-boiled. Poached, scrambled, shirred, and baked in cream, we celebrated the wide possibility of eggs. By Easter, Zoe was old enough to eat her own eggs but she didn't like them scrambled. By age three, she was old enough to order them her own way. Unlike us, she prefers her eggs worldly: the savory scallion pancakes my friend Okim makes, the egg in fried rice, the lemon custard passed down by her Swedish great-grandmother. She likes the egg in Japanese tempura and the hollandaise egg. Once, the world was hospital-room-small for her and now it is global-big. We follow the egg as it leaves the room and takes us on a world tour by Zoe.

Eggs, in all their permutations, are always turning into something else. Even a broken mess of eggs has the potential to become something delicious. Take a stringy mass of unfertilized eggs. Crack them hard. Beat them aggressively. Cook them over too-high heat. Even eggs scrambled by a mediocre cook are edible. But you'll get better. Take your first shot and then revise and revise. Ask your friends for some help. Consult cookbooks from across the globe. This cooking thing is important business; all these broken eggs. We have to communicate better if we're going to put them back together—or, at least, if we're going to do something worthy of all this breakage.

My husband's nickname is Egg, and, as female-made as the egg is, there's something about the soft, impressionable inside and the hard, protective outside of egg that doesn't signal "female" so much as "potential," and, you, dear egg, I'm pretty certain that the world isn't possible without you.

Why we break the things we love the most

Eggs like their fragility. Little planets full of life go out of their way to show their cracks, their fault lines. Examining their flaws reveals their tensile strength. What does not kill me, etcetera, etcetera. Calcium swarms to heal the fissure, prevent fracture. Hold an egg up to your eye: imperfections swirl gray rivers. Scratch your finger across it—it's as perfect as it ever was, as beautiful as a planet, heaving with life, stronger than it looks yet still likely to break.

So many kinds of eggs. Ostrich. Robin. Dinosaur. Hummingbird. Turkey. Chicken. Salmon. Platypus. Rattlesnake and flycatcher. Northern flicker and rabbit. Even mammals have eggs, though on the inside: ovaries tossing out eggs like cigarette butts from a car window. The mammal's interior planets round the stomach rather than the nest. Perhaps the mammal's eggs seem less fragile, protected as they are through muscle and fat. This makes them nonetheless precious. They break too, these internal eggs.

I am not so attached to my eggs, or should I say, they are not so attached to me. I drop one every month and let it go ten days later. The results are runny as yolk, full of proteins and lost possibilities but not one of those possibilities is a frittata. Chicken eggs, post extrusion, are much more full of potential. I've made frittatas with sausage and broccoli, with mushrooms and cheese, omelets with asparagus and omelets with Denver, scrambled eggs with American cheese cooked on low to keep the proteins from seizing up. Eggs in cookies and eggs in cakes. A dozen eggs separated, whites whipped into a fury, folded back into their yolks, risen in a soufflé. But I like eggs best whole. Hard-boiled. I poach eggs in chicken broth, which seems both a deep bow and a deep "fuck you" to the hen.

My favorite recipe is the one that my friend Rebecca brought with her all the way from Los Angeles to meet me to camp on the Mogollon Rim above Sycamore Canyon. Although not part of the Grand Canyon, the Sycamore Canyon's elemental construction comes from the same planetary insides—Colorado Plateau. Navajo Sandstone, limestone, Kaibab rock.

Rebecca and I hadn't spoken in five years. And then we did. And then we ate ham cream. What I recall from the recipe is this:

Sauté onion in a pan. Add cream. Add ham. Reduce. Add spinach. Pour into ramekins. Crack an egg in. Bake for 12–15 minutes.

We had no oven in which to bake our ham cream on the Mogollon Rim. I rolled my eyes that Rebecca brought such a complicated recipe to cook on a camping stove—part of the reason we didn't speak for five years. She has a tendency to complicate everything. So do I. Two complicators make a mess of a nest.

Still, we were talking now and moving forward with the ham cream. We sautéed the onions in a sauté pan over the rattling burner of the Coleman stove. We added the cream and ham. Turned off the burner. Let the ham steep. Lighting the stove again required matches and delicate balancing of the too-hot pan in one of her hands. I held the pan. She lit the burner. Division of labor we had always been good at. We both burned our hands, her burn sharp and biting, mine broad and deepening. I could have made a metaphor out of it, but metaphors lead to fighting. I wanted us to be happy. We had so many eggs to go.

We cracked eight eggs and added them to the pan. This is the important part: one egg per person. Who was here? How had Rebecca and I—friends since eighth grade, arguing about which came first, man or woman, art or science, whose boyfriend was the lamest, how to make art and money, if art was functional was it still art, how to stay friends across ten western states—managed to bring anyone else camping with us? Our husbands and our kids, patient as we stirred the onions. We cracked the eggs, opened them into the hot pan. Put a lid on it. Scraped the ham and spinach, eggs still whole onto our plates.

How do you want your eggs?

Perfect.

There are reasons to repair a broken friendship. One of them is egg poached in cream.

"Why do you want kids?" my one-time student and now friend, Lydia, asked during the gap of time that Rebecca and I weren't speaking. I needed someone else to ask the obvious questions. Not that the question was obvious, Rebecca never had asked obvious questions, nor did Lydia. But the answer seemed obvious. Lydia didn't want kids. I had always wanted kids. How do you describe a want? About as easily as you fulfill it. Desire isn't easy. It's a vacuum, a black hole—an empty egg in which someone has poked a hole and let the mucousy dreams drip out.

Culturally conditioned to want kids? Sure. Biologically determined to have kids? Maybe. Romantically deluded about the joys of having kids? Absolutely. On nights when I couldn't sleep, I lay in my bed and dreamed about a tiny fetal head tucking under my ribs. I could imagine the baby turning more slowly that a planet, more life-filled than a rainforest. Maybe it was years of having sex, having near misses and not misses and not having babies that accumulated in those empty spaces like rabbits of desire. Ghost rabbits.

Practically, I weighed the problem of having kids. That they might get in the way of the plan to make a living making art. The carbon their baby feet would print. The fear of them dying. The fear of the world killing them. The loss of free time and sanity and sleep, even when they became teenagers— especially when they became teenagers, and I would have to wait and wait late into the night for them to crawl back through the window through which they had escaped. Wanting not to sleep seemed like a bad wish. Wanting not to die seemed melodramatic. Although immortality seems more guaranteed through babies than through art. Why did I want kids? Some things are best understood when contemplating their opposite.

Not having kids felt like the end of the world.

I should have a scene here, an image of me in the bathroom, looking at the one lonely line on the pregnancy test. I should have an image of me in stirrups, the doctors shaking their heads glumly. I should have a scene with a test tube or maybe one of me going to the Baby Gap and a pair of booties while saying to the wind gods, Please fill these with something besides yourself, wind. But those images are pervasive. You've seen them before in play-by-play blogs where every blip on the fertility thermometer is recorded. When the basal body temperature falls, the comment section sighs collectively. There is love to be found in some comment sections. Isn't that enough? Why should you want a child? Oh interrogative question mark. Why are you shaped like a hook? You keep leaving me hopeful that I can catch this desire. Conveying empty is like trying to convey a promise. I will be here for you. Who will believe you? Where will you be? I thought we were going camping. Why should you have any faith?

I complicate the exterior, paint ornately on the shell, tap gently against the egg for good luck. If I can't get anything substantial from the egg itself, I will distract myself with the beauty of a scramble or a Fabergé. I will make something out of nothing.

For distraction, I look for beauty. For faith, I look for signs. Things that help me believe. Signs that convey distantly, like I saw a hawk this morning which means I will get some good news about my book later this afternoon. Rebecca saw a falcon and her gallery, LA Louver, called that very afternoon.

We optimists take birds as signs to human endeavor because, at the end of the world, only the birds can hold out until the scorched earth settles down. I feel bad, hanging all this hope around the neck of birds, both the fulfillment of pedestrian, even petty wishes, and the hope of their eternal survival. I forgive myself my weightiness in advance. They know I'm only joking. Ask the passenger pigeon. Ask the passenger pigeon's unfertilized egg.

In the time between morning and afternoon, all possibility is wide and open, waiting like a door for good news to walk in. I do not like the signs that convey immediately. The sign of a menstrual period is unmistakable. You try to ignore the tug on your ovary, the twist of muscle under your belly button. Your belly button makes you think of your mother. The thought of her reminds you that infertility cannot be hereditary. Your mother, though, was twenty-five when she got pregnant with you and you are thirty-one. You are on your way to your friend Rebecca's for a breakfast she's hosting on Christmas Eve. This is the past so you are still speaking to her but you are not happy that she is making Egg Stuff. Egg Stuff is an even worse name for something like egg strudel. Eggs and cooked sausage layered between yesterday's stale bread. Soggy bread is disgusting. My own mother would terrorize me on days I stayed home sick from school as she ate toast soaked in milk. If I'd gone to school, she seemed to be saying as the milk seeped into the bread's natural gaps, threatening to turn it back into dough, I wouldn't have to witness this toast apocalypse. Worse. Mush. Worse. Milky mush. Egg stuff is another horrible example of soggy bread. Eggs ruining bread. Bread ruining eggs. Overnight. In the fridge. A day's worth of soaking. I could feel the bread collapsing between my fingers. The word "moist" comes to mind. Moist is a word, Emily, Rebecca's friend and now my friend, hates. She would also be at the breakfast. She is a vegetarian. Vegetarians can get out of eating anything. If I had two dreams in life it is to have kids and be a vegetarian but perhaps I am constitutionally ill designed for either.

For Christmas Eve breakfast, none of us talk about having kids. None of us ever did. We are thirty. Thirty feels young. So young. Like as young as nineteen. Only people who had children in their twenties can tell the difference between nineteen and thirty.

That morning, after making the bread suffer all night long in eggy, milky wetness, Rebecca cooks the Egg Stuff in the oven for forty minutes. When she cuts into the casserole, it isn't soggy. The bread, though possibly moist, is not wet. The top is even crunchy. The sausage tastes delicious because it is sausage (what does Emily eat? Not moist bread. Does Rebecca use vegetarian sausage?) The eggs have turned the bread to a kind of soufflé. Humble beginnings, delicious puffed entrée. I wish it were Christmas Eve morning every day although I continue to avoid milk toast and bread crusts left in the bottom of the kitchen sink and there were years, whole years, during the time when Rebecca did not speak to me, during the time I willed my own personal eggs to shift into high gear, that I did not eat a single bite of once-soggy bread.

Things that you might think are signs that are not signs: Soggy bread is not necessarily a sign of soggy breakfast. A late period is not necessarily a sign of pregnancy. A raised piece of humus is not necessarily a mushroom. When I walk through the forest, looking at the ground for mushrooms and for owl pellets, if I see an owl pellet I look up. I have never seen an owl in the forest. I look for them anyway. What do I want with a predator bird? Perhaps they are strong enough to slough off my wishing weight. Don't die, planet. Bring me a baby, bird. Perhaps wish-birds are the great equalizer. Staving off the end of the world is always, finally, a selfish hope. Baby, lie to me. Come live in my belly so the world can go on. Bird. Bring me a baby. Mushroom. Bring me an egg. I will make an omelet. Sometimes, an egg is not a sign of anything except breakfast.

There are a lot of ends of the world: Avian flu, melting glaciers, fracked water, Ebola, asteroids, listeria. Listeria's not one of them? Well, it should be, because if you're pregnant you're told not to eat deli meats for the risk they carry of listeria that would abort your fetus—which would be a small end of a very small world. Ends of the world are scaleable. Human egg. Ostrich egg. Dinosaur egg.

How do I do this? I want to ask Rebecca but this is during the time we aren't talking. I'm shouting into a hollowed-out egg. Echo. Echo. Where did I put that goopy yolk? Maybe I can at least turn this white into a sad meringue. I try to send a message. I revise it. I delete it. I try again.

I tried talking to my eggs. I tried poking them with my fists. I tried rubbing progesterone cream onto them. Skin and muscle and that yellow belly fat they say will kill you were in my way. I was as satisfied as a dinosaur—as in, not very. These eggs fulfilled neither me, nor their destiny. Maybe they had been scrambled. Maybe I had sent too many subliminal "don't be fertilized, don't be fertilized" messages to them over the years. Maybe subliminal messages are the only kind they hear, carried subterranean from brain to stem to nerve to egg. Maybe they got the message and wouldn't forgive me. Maybe now that I wanted them, they had all the power. Like any wish, it seems emptier once it is spoken. Big rounds of air coming out of my mouth like thought bubbles or balloons.

I chant to my eggs. I envision a zygote. I find a quotation. I paint a picture of what I think I want to want. There was an egg. There were many eggs. They came first. They went away. Trying to chase a lost egg is like trying to catch an escaped hen. No one will sit down for you.

Which came first: my fear of the end of the world or my fear of the end of me?

Let's make something out of all this potential energy. Perhaps then we can answer the question. Let's paint a picture. First there was a woman. Then she had a friend. Then she lost her friend. Then she had a child. Then, she revised her story. She no longer believed the version she'd been telling herself—that Rebecca loved to argue more than she loved her. Instead, she wrote, "I like to argue too. I had a baby. If there is anyone in the world I want to know she exists, it is you. You're the one who always believed with me that art was something, made from nothing. I would like you to know that I always did believe. I had faith."

When her friend came back, that friend came back with two children, a carton of eggs, a chunk of ham, and some onion. Perhaps deciding what to make for breakfast had been the problem all along.

When Rebecca paints, she paints with oil, not egg tempera. She paints in her studio, while in her kitchen she makes a lemon cake into which she has folded four binding eggs. She plans to share the cake. She takes the cake to the gallery owner. The gallery owner offers the prospective buyer a piece of cake. Rebecca doesn't tell her about her eggs, the number of them or how many she has cracked. She doesn't mention her kids. No one needs an artist who also has a brood. It's no one's business what we do with our eggs; that's why their shells are opaque. No one is allowed to look in. No one's looking back. But everyone is thinking, inside, inside, inside. That's where the art lives. There's a whole lot of potential in that egg. Everyone wants to hold it. Everyone loves the beginning of something even if they don't know where the beginning will go. Eggs are the beginning because they are air and because they are glue, which is how we've kept it together, off and on, for so long. Alternating currents. Silence and speech. Uterus full and uterus empty. Potential potential potential. Chicken.

Rotten eggs

You would eat a pickled egg, yes? So the thousand-year-old egg isn't much different. It's also known as a century egg and even that is pushing it. Maybe a few months, max. This century egg is a duck egg preserved in clay and salt, sometimes with quicklime and ash, but basically a kind of pickling preservation along the lines of kimchi. You eat kimchi, right?

The century egg, aka the preserved egg, tastes like an old egg: flavors of horse urine, cat pee, overwrought sauerkraut, with a lingering bouquet of graveyard, tomb, catacomb. Raw eggs are packed in salt and clay for six weeks. These alkaline substances raise the pH inside the egg, making it safe but also full of ammonia smells—which is a kind of rotten but in a good, or at least safely consumable, way.

My refrigerator might be going bad. I began to suspect something when I could smell the chicken through its packaging. They don't wrap chicken in plastic only to keep it pretty on the shelves. The plastic helps prevent the chicken rotting, and, barring that, helps prevent the smell of chicken as it rots. I still cooked the chicken. I also had a raw turkey breast that was beginning to smell like flesh. I cooked that, too. On the grill. It didn't cook all the way through. I cut the raw parts off and put them in the possibly defunct fridge.

And then I cooked those raw parts the next morning for breakfast. I didn't die so it's 100 percent not rotten; maybe preserved by stomach acid is the better term.

My kids don't say it so much; they're more the "Not it," "You're it," types. But I did say it when I was a kid and possibly sometimes still do when Erik and I are running to get today's mail—"Last one there is a rotten egg"—because the mail is exciting and the eggs are always: from the minute they fall from the hootchie of the hen, also known as "the vent," beginning their slow rot. The shell acts as a kind of protector, like the wrappers around the chicken and the turkey, but stronger and, until it's way too late, odor free.

It doesn't seem quite fair, when racing your friends, to be considered "rotten" just because you're slow. Plus, how many times does the person who says "Last one there is a rotten egg" get a head start, making it halfway to the mailbox before the words are out of his mouth? And, what happens when the slow nonracer shrugs her shoulders and says, "That's fine. I'm rotten." How rotten is she? Game spoiler? Or just a wise person who knows the game itself is an ancient one and being rotten isn't the worst thing in the world? Rotten is mostly a game of point of view.

The egg came first

In the beginning, there was a great, cosmic egg; so goes the creation story of the Dogon people, a tribe from what is now modern-day Mali. The idea of the cosmic egg is the only easy part of this story. After that, things get sticky: Amma, a male god, shook and shook the egg until eight seeds, called words, fertilized the egg. Those words—since shaking is generative and fertilizing creative—joined together to create two pairs of twins called Nommo. These were androgynous beings, each one containing the spirit of each gender. But, perhaps because of the shaking or perhaps because of the gendered nature of words themselves, gender took root. One of the male twins, sometimes named Yurungu, sometimes called Ogo, wanted out of that egg to make a world for himself. He abandoned his twin, who would suffer for his rebellion, as all twins suffer for each other. In Ogo's escape, he tore off some of the placenta. That placenta, twirling in space, became earth. As Ogo sailed through space, he realized how cold and silent it was out there. He wanted to return to his twin, to repair the broken egg, but once the egg is cracked, it's hard to put it back together again. Note Humpty Dumpty. Note real eggs. Ogo, ostracized.

Ogo can't repair the egg so he takes his loneliness out on earth. He procreates and procreates with this earth, a kind of incest that Amma cannot abide. Amma fixes everything by rending asunder his twin, throwing her into the universe, creating a sun, humans, animals, and two stars, Sirius B and the lesser-known Sirius A. Amma turns Ogo into a fox, family *Canidae*, who learns to speak. He tries to communicate with humans but he is not welcome by any of the villagers. Not everyone wants to hear what you are saying, especially if you're talking about having sex with yourself. Or your twin. In another version of the myth, Amma himself has sex with his creation, the earth. The earth, hermaphroditic like his other creations, has a clitoris. Amma, threatened by the penis-like appendage, circumcises earth. Gender is enforced, everything falls apart, everyone tries to put Humpty Dumpty together again; binaries are created, lines are drawn, babies are made. The world is a mess but at least it exists, and the mess gives people something to write home about.[1]

My own creation myth involves no incest unless you count neighbors as family. I was eleven when my best friend's brother had sex with me. I tell this story often—too often. It's embarrassing, really. But this is why I tell it. It has become my creation story. Before that time, my universe seemed well ordered. My dad had a good job as a vice-president for drilling research; he raised roses in his spare time. My mom volunteered with the League of Women Voters. She was the first one in the city to separate her garbage into recyclables. My twin sisters were my best friends. I carried one on my front and one on my back, like a horse and a goat, chivvying Quixote on my back, Odysseus hanging to my front. But then, when I was eleven, something astral tore through that universe. After that, my parents divorced. My sisters and I fled to different corners of the country. The roses died. Blood, as in menstrual, flowed—I waited for it to set some kind of order, but the periods came sometimes, surprisingly, never like clockwork. If only I could stuff my eggs back in.

It's not true, I suspect, that what happened changed the course of my life so dramatically but it's my creation myth, so it's the one I tell. I don't like to write about it but I do like to write. Each word an eggshell, each typing stroke a piece of glue. Somehow, I'll put this egg back together.

In India, the Vedic creation myth tells of warming oceans, a legendary kind of climate change. The seas sweated and roiled in the heat of a fertile moment, one wave smacking against another like two hawks in the air, flinging their cloacae toward each other, inseminating as much by wind as by body. It took nine months for that egg to gestate fully, but finally a golden egg was born from the seas. From this giant egg Prajapati, the creator, emerged.

This is a sexy egg, born by rocking in high seas and salty sweat. Unlike the violence of the Dogon myth, this Vedic myth seems if not consensual, at least chancy and inevitable.[2]

Brian Evenson, author of *Father of Lies*, a book about a wayward Mormon bishop who molests children in his Mormon ward, once asked me how to poach an egg. I told him, it's easy. Don't let the waters boil too high. Use fresh eggs from the farmer's market. It is not hard to poach an egg.

I wanted to ask Brian Evenson, how do you write stories like what you wrote about the father and husband and church member who molested neighborhood kids, or the one I'm writing about a bishop drawing one of his congregates into his office, asking her to explain why she wore such short skirts, letting her know he'd heard how far she'd let Jacob go with her in the primary school classroom, asking her to listen to him because he held the priesthood and the rule of the church was the rule of the male and he sees her looking at him, nervously, maybe sexily, maybe that biting of the lip is a kind of acquiescence and he thinks maybe the best way to purify her thoughts is by washing her clitoris with his tongue which is male and therefore holy. He asks her with an authority vested in him by the power of God and the Holy Ghost to sit on his lap and at first it is just simple touching over the skirt but the skirt is short and the underwear is damp, which is another kind of invitation. He needs to adjust her to touch her more deeply. He leans her forward and now there's room for more than just fingers. All the while he's telling her that this is what God intended by creation, man and woman, once divided and opposed, now united.

How do your write this, I wanted to ask, without arousing your reader? Or do you want them aroused? But that seemed beyond the bounds of the conversation. I didn't want to break the rules of propriety by interjecting weird words. Instead, I asked him if he had success with the poached eggs. He said, "yes, thanks," which I took as a positive answer to both questions.

In the Chinese myth of Pangu, inside a giant cosmic egg Pangu grows ten feet a day. Although things are disorganized inside the egg in the beginning, as he gets larger, Pangu separates the sky and earth within the egg. He separates everything into its opposing parts: male and female, wet and dry, light and dark, white and yolk, yin and yang, because, paradoxically, taxonomy is the first step of creation. You have to know your constituent parts before you can mix things up again. After 18,000 years, the egg hatches. Pangu dies in the birthing, but from Pangu's sweat rain and oceans were made. His eyes became the sun and moon. His kneecaps turned Himalayan. From his nose flowed the Yellow River. His chest flattened into the plains of Mongolia. His hair bristled tall rice that reached toward the clouds. The rice drew the clouds down. His cheeks became the shore. Everything that is comes from an egg.[3]

The egg cannot stay perfect and whole if you want more of anything. For life to happen, you need unrest, dismay, disorder. Then, you spend the rest of your life trying to get it back in order, a kind of forced revision to your original origin story. The unfertilized chicken egg is half white, half yolk, but you don't know that until you open it. Crack the egg and you've unleashed the binary.

Then the binary spends the night, rolling around in bed sheeting, trying to get back to the singular, the unified. A couple, coupled, stomach to stomach, breast to breast, legs wrapped tightly around each other, approximates the shape of an egg. If they could stay there forever, tab A inserted into slot B, maybe order would be restored. But then, even what we call sex might get a little boring.

It's not until after the egg has cracked and you are floating singularly through space that you realize everyone else is marching two by two and you, creator of creation myths, are on your own. Who doesn't long for the egg before Ogo broke the shell? Who, being divided into opposing parts, doesn't miss the chaos of the whole complete egg?

As the sun set along Laguna Beach, my parents in front of me, my twin sisters following behind, I walked with my shadow. This shadow was a man: taller than me, kinder, more patient. I fell in love. I tried to hold hands with him but I couldn't feel any strength around my fingers. Still, in the shadows, I saw two hands, clasped together. Our heads grew long across the shore. Our feet, and then our pelvises, became submerged in the water. Out there, in the sea, we would conceive our child of brine—from the egg made from wave meeting wave, our shadow child would be born. She would be too small to see as she swung between us. One, two, three, swing!

There are four sequential worlds in the Navajo creation story. The first world is dark, covered by four oceans; an island marks the center where ants, dragonflies, locusts, and beetles live around and inside and on the bark of one single tree. There are four clouds. The clouds commingle, as do waves as do birds as do mammals, pressing what bodies they possess against each other, turning inside each other, rolling as the storms boil. When the black and white clouds come together, they create man. When the blue and yellow clouds come together, they create woman. The woman tries to reach the man three times. On the fourth try, she finds him. He invites her to live with him. She agrees. As they sit by the fire of their newfound home, a coyote, family *Canidae*, visits. He says he was born from an egg. He brings witchcraft to the world, the first thing people need. Witchcraft is magic and so is fire and so are words. They sat by the fire, telling stories of the second, third, and fourth world that by so telling came to be.

In telling your creation myth, you can shape it anyway you want; like an egg-rich dough, you hold it in your hands, away from you. It is other. You, as teller, stand apart from the story. You try out a few words. "There was a mattress in the basement." You watch your audience's face as it drops, lifts, the forehead wrinkles, the cheeks slacken, tighten. This is almost as much body response as you get from having sex. You move closer to your listener's face. "I wanted to hold his hand at church but he wouldn't let me. Except on the way home. Then he placed my hand where he thought it fit best." You would kiss your listener's face if that would mean you could tell a different story. But you come from where you come. The coyote, in this story, is magical, but even more dangerous than the fox. You move closer to your listener's face but she steps back. You have wilderness inside you, you who have stepped outside of the normal social order, you who cracked the egg too early. The listener steps back for you fear you may bite—or worse, that you may be contagious, that the age of consent will slip backward. The clitoris is no longer a diagram in the book *Our Bodies, Ourselves*, but a defiant body. The defiant body should be removed and the noisy voice should become quiet, says Amma. Your creation myth is not their creation myth. They'd prefer to hear again the one about the ocean.

We all tried to keep it together. Abrupt, even violent, transitions can lead to big changes but abrupt transitions can also lead to a stringy mess of unfertilized futures, unfulfilled potential. My dad tried Antabuse to stop drinking. My mom tried Optifast to stop eating. My twin sisters tried to be good—gymnastics, soccer, dance, piano. My award-winning sisters each carried a bit of the shell back to the homestead and tried to piece it together. Therapists told us that alcoholics are absent in mind even if they are present in body. Our father, though home, wasn't really with us, the therapist told us. That's why we went looking for love in the wrong places (or too early), trying to replace that absence. We tried to make this story work as a rationale to our longing but dad had been always there, with us, even if he was a little drunk. When that story didn't stick, the therapist used Prozac as glue. I tried repairing the family, my reputation, by getting straight A's, being home by exactly nine o'clock, ten o'clock on weekends. I was never one second late but the egg timer had already rung. The egg was already overcooked. If you leave an egg on the sidewalk on a hot day, the sun bakes it anyway. The story of a broken childhood solidified. It's hard to revise in the past tense.

Truly, the only thing that helped was walking the neighbor's French poodle, family *Canidae*, around and around the block a hundred times a day, circularity reinscribing the meaning. Also, going to the zoo. The animals in the zoo made sense—zebras next to seals, polar bears near camels, kangaroos by elephants. This was evidence of what happens when you try to reorder the cracked and rent-asunder world: cages and mixed-up species. The zoo smelled of manure and of popcorn. Humans disorganizing the world, trying to make it look organized. I felt at home there.

In the Orphic Greek creation story, Nyx, the bird with black wings, known as the darkness itself, commingled with wind. She laid a golden egg upon which she sat for ages until within, life began to stir and the seas began to rock and the volcanoes began to shake. The egg began to crack. Out of this egg, Phanes, the hermaphrodite, was born. The hermaphrodite commingled with itself to spawn the Gods whose names and capriciousness we know better.

Would we be satisfied being alone if we could mate with ourselves? So peaceful: a duplicate of ourselves exactly reflecting ourselves, like the little girl on the beach, a product of self and shadow? No binaries. The stories would have no conflict, so there would be no stories.

Or would it be the worst kind of incest? The most inbred of the inbreeding—so much self, so much narcissism. A story of a story of a story? A matryoshka doll. A Fabergé egg. We'd dress up the image in the mirror to make ever more beautiful everything we wanted to see there but maybe wasn't. Fabergé concocted ever smaller, ever more complicated surprises to be found inside the egg, but the yolk itself? Never fertilized.

For years I told myself a version of this story until it began to grow like anything with a genetic pool of one grows: Once you are no longer virgin, that egg is cracked. There's no repairing that hymen-y shell. What could happen: Your mom will call you slut. Your sisters will go to a different high school than you. Your dad will drink vodka out of the trunk of a car. Your destiny is sealed. You'll probably get pregnant at sixteen, live in a cheap apartment on 2nd South where the other prostitutes live. You'll probably raise that kid on Coca-Cola and Lucky Charms. "Man hands misery onto man," wrote Phillip Larkin. You'll write the verse over and over again in your journal.

But as coastal shelves go deeper and darker, other geographic shelves rise. Sometimes, you can climb out of Utah, out of the past, out of your shell. When I left Salt Lake City for Reed College, I expected there to be a thousand people just like me. We would all listen to Crass, wearing *The Feeding of the 5,000* T-shirts. We would take acid and try to triangulate the distances of stars. But boys were still boys there, and girls were still seen as broken or unbroken. As one of the broken, I stood and watched from my dorm-room window the pack of Reed dogs, family *Candiae*, roam the front lawn. The dogs had a boundlessness that I thought I might have but couldn't quite access. I didn't know then that everyone was broken and most everyone could heal themselves—eventually.

In the earliest Egyptian myths, there were eight gods called the Ogdoad, four male and four female representations of primeval water, the infinitude of water, the wildness of nature, and the darkness of the deep ocean. Like any evenly numbered group of women and men, disorder happened and sex happened, the seas roiled and commingled, converged, piling up enough mud and dirt to create a mound big enough for a celestial to lay a golden egg. That egg contained Ra, the Sun God. The Egyptians believed that he was swallowed every night by the Sky Goddess Nut and was reborn every morning.

A lesson in destruction and creation, every day. Rebound.

I dated an English major. We met in fiction class. I wrote a story that began, "She ate ice cream in hopes of getting pregnant." He wrote a story called "The Inside Passage" about a cruise to Alaska and which contained, like all good stories, some hint of incest. He told me that girls who were molested have a hard time trusting men. He said that children of alcoholics are always insecure because they were never sure if their parent loved the booze more than the kid. He was probably right, but as a survivor of childhood sexual experience and an alcoholic parent, I didn't trust him and wasn't sure I was worthy of his love anyway. As a sign of our hope for the future, we got a cat but a cat is not a baby. We wrote poems to each other instead of conceiving. I loved the idea that he loved me for my words but then he wrote a letter longer than any of his stories to a redhead who was twenty-five years old and still a virgin because who does not best love an egg still whole?

In Tahiti, the god Taaroa was conceived inside the cosmic egg. When he broke out, the egg became the sky and he himself became the earth. Who would choose to be the body that all stories are played out upon? Who wouldn't prefer the dreaminess of sky? Maybe there is something to be said for, and of, the messiness of the terrestrial.

One of my good friends, Ander, also a writer, but also not like me, once told me that he admired the way I raised my kids because I wasn't trying to recreate a perfect version of my own broken childhood. No, I said, I'm sure I will break my kids' childhoods in new and original ways. Then I wrote stories about my daughter who said the word "hawk" instead of "dinner" and my son who begged to wear cowboy boots even though the cowboy boots were on his feet, in an attempt to preserve them in my writing of their whole-egg status.

The Mande people, like the Dogon, believe that two pairs of twins were seeded inside the egg. Each set of twin a male and female. These were the first people from whom all people are generated.

If I could choose to make a world where these two kids, not twins but brother and sister, could appreciate different bodies without penetrating them, could compare body parts without seeing one as opposed to the other, who will wait for each other to finish the other's story, who do not fight over who gets the last Oreo, well, maybe this could be a different kind of world. But of course, everyone fights over the last Oreo.

These two kids of mine, though, have, when I'm not looking, cut an Oreo exactly in half and shared it without breaking anything, without even speaking. They give the crumbs to the dog. He is silent too. There are innate understandings that don't require words.

In the Bon religion in Tibet, two immortals commingle to turn spirit matter into three eggs. The golden egg produced a golden arrow, gendered male, with turquoise feathers. The turquoise egg produced a turquoise arrow, gendered female, with golden feathers. And the white egg? An ungendered golden spindle. Many pointy objects—feather, arrow, spindle—have been spawned: a sperm-meets-egg archetype on the road to reproduction. Or maybe the feathers, arrows, spindles break the white egg, leaving a gooey, messy creation on the would-be earth's floor.

I cannot tell if this is a violent story, a sexy story, or a story of how binaries get made. The story has more color than most. Maybe it's a commentary on art and light. Maybe the arrows and the spindles aren't gendered at all. A utopia with the possibility of consensual sex.

My daughter came home from her fifth grade maturation program yesterday. I took her brother to their grandma's so she could ask me any questions alone. We took the dog for a walk so she didn't have to look me in the eye. She told me about the antisex-abuse video they watched, where a soccer coach wanted to take naked pictures of one of the kids on his team to show "how he had grown," about a friend at a party who put his hand up a girl's shirt and started to rub her back, about a neighbor who asked one of the girls at the sleepover to come to his bedroom, about an uncle who put his hands down his niece's pants. She told the stories with hugely shocked eyes. Although I was not surprised by the stories, I made my face reflect her shock. What I was surprised by was the fact that in fifth grade, in this very conservative state, they were willing to talk about how to say no and get help, so young, but maybe also just in time.

The first step to keeping eggs whole is to see the egg for what it is, even if you're not looking your daughter in the eye. To hold it apart from the self and see the story as separate from you. Getting outside the egg isn't easy. Humans are particularly bad at it but maybe it is the one thing writers have going for them. Writers love the externalized egg, full of creation, disaster, potential, excitement, and story.

I asked Zoe why she might not want to have sex too early. She said, "Because you don't want to have a baby when you're sixteen and you don't have a job or have anywhere to live and you can't get married."

I asked, "Why else not?"

"Because it's weird? And I'd have to tell you?"

"Well, telling me would mean that you took time to think about it." I said, "If you can talk to me about it, then you're probably in control and if you're in control, it is a story that you get to choose, not the story the world has given you. If you can talk to me about it, before you do it, then you can write your own story. Which you should do. Because you're a good writer." One nice thing about a whole egg is you can hold it in your hand, and look at it from every angle. It will take forever to make decisions this way, turning the egg over and over in your hand, but possibly this is what I'm going for.

You are not the egg, I want to tell her; you just tell its story. But that is a myth, too. We are always our egg.

The dog pulled hard on the leash. "Zorra (family *Canidae*, Spanish for fox, gendered female), stop it!" Zoe yelled at her. Zoe's voice is high and but authoritative. Zorra is just a puppy but she understood the word "stop." I looked at them both— grateful at the word stop and at the stopping. And grateful for Zorra's walking needs. It took getting out of the house, away from everyone else—the chance to look straight ahead or bother with the dog—to be able to say anything at all. Without the egg, there would be no becoming, but without the dog, there wouldn't be a way to talk about what it's like to become.

In the *Kalevala*, the Finnish national epic, there is a myth of the world being created from the fragments of an egg laid by a diving duck on the knee of Ilmatar, goddess of the air:

> One egg's lower half transformed
> And became the earth below,
> And its upper half transmuted
> And became the sky above;
> From the yolk the sun was made,
> Light of day to shine upon us;
> From the white the moon was formed,
> Light of night to gleam above us;
> All the colored brighter bits
> Rose to be the stars of heaven
> And the darker crumbs changed into
> Clouds and cloudlets in the sky.

The Finnish myth may be my favorite because it's not what came out of the egg, separate from the egg. The whole egg, not separate from its shell, becomes the world. There is no order without disorder, they're not even binary positions. There was no beginning, just transformation of material, substances re-seen. A yolk looks like the sun. The white is the moon. The metaphors move us from small personal disaster to large, global crumminess. And then the crumbs reproduce and become clouds in the sky. Large global reparations remind us of the time we knit ourselves a new eggshell and called it our myth and we loved it even though the oceans roiled and the earth quaked and fell apart. The oceans quieted, eventually. The earth, stretched, now lies calm. The earth comes back together. Every morning, the dog, family *Canidae*, barks to be let out, telling us to wake to tell again the story of how the egg—even if it had cracked and broken the night before—rises whole and completely itself in the morning.

Experiment with eggs by making a hollandaise in the time of global warming

Lecithin is a protein in egg yolks that helps to make an emulsion. Emulsions are things like salad dressing and mayonnaise, gravies, and the five mother sauces: béchamel, velouté, hollandaise, tomato, and espagnole. The lecithin holds them together. Lecithin is a kind of leviathan. It is a fish of a molecule. A busybody of a protein that likes to put its nose in a cell of water and its tail in a cell of fat, bringing the sauce together. It's a matchmaker of water and oil, preventing the oil droplets from pooling together. Oil droplets are Romeo and Juliet. We have to keep them apart if we want this lemon juice to hold up its heavier, fatter lover with its tiny, slippery hands.

Of the mother sauces, only hollandaise uses eggs instead of a roux to bring things together. You have to break up the egg itself first, separate white from yolk. If you have a hard time separating eggs, the Internet provides a video of a water bottle sucking the yolk into its mouth, leaving the white behind. Picture a popping sound like the kind the fish make when they need a lot of oxygen and have to force the water faster over their gills, or the sound of a whale bringing to surface only his blowhole. In a hollandaise, air is not your friend (leave air and eggs for meringues and soufflés—the whites, the whites! Shut up. This is a yolk story, heavy as water). Try to ignore the fossil fuels it took to make your plastic bottle. Disregard that this plastic will, most likely, end up in the plastic garbage patch that spans the size of Texas, swirls in the Pacific Ocean. Maybe the plastic will meet its mate there. Who are you to keep them apart?

Remember, you're a matchmaker, trying to arrange the right marriage and hollandaise is, of all things, moral, truly righteous. You can add hollandaise to cold salmon or hot asparagus. You can double-dip your egg eating and make a Benedict over which you pour the hot hollandaise onto hot poached egg and the difference in egg here is more distinct than a Capulet or a Montague.

To make a good hollandaise, you need good balance more than a good story. Juliet and Romeo will not suffice. Hollandaise is the wisdom of the mother, not the rush of the youth. Separating the yolks takes balance. Producing the lecithin takes patience. Pouring the butter into the egg and lemon mixture is the kind of equation that makes for healthy, bountiful seas. Not too much lemony acid. Don't let the temperature get too hot. If you want hollandaise—and your ocean—to be productive, you have to know when too warm is too warm.

Hollandaise marries best with almost every kind of fish but, as Romeo goes, so doth the bigeye tuna. The cod. The halibut. Even the salmon, whose own blend of water and fat make the fish canonical and invincible, a hollandaise itself, until it breaks into water and egg as hard and pliable as plastic.

How to cook a planet

Recipe for a planet:

1 singularity
1 expanding universe
1 pile of space dust
1 cup disobedience
4 cups punishment

Swirl ingredients around either big-bangily or invented Godily. Mix to combine. Shake to ensure combination. Fold in matter with antimatter, gas with gas, gravity with electronic charge. Proportion, balance, and chemical reactions are all it takes to make a cake—or, in this case, a primordial soup; a little more mixing, some surprising hydrogens catching some sweet carbons. A hook-up for the weekend resulting in an amoeba that is, in some ways, an egg. From the amoeba-egg hatches a two-celled chicken that produces another egg. It's always the egg that came first. Before the egg, there was only soup.

Recipe for soufflé:

4 large egg yolks
5 egg whites
1 package frozen spinach, defrosted

4 tablespoons butter
4 tablespoons flour
1 cup grated gruyère
1 cup scalded milk

Soufflé might be the best creation story. Like these myths, you have to separate the eggs, egg from ocean, wet from dry, hydrogen from oxygen, in order to make something new. To make soufflé you must separate at least four eggs. Maybe six. Make a béchamel, which is really just a roux with milk (and onion poked with cloves if you're really serious, which I am not). Add the egg yolks and cheese to the roux. Whip the egg whites until frothy. Fold in the whites, an egg at a time. Put in oven and watch the creation lift toward the clouds. Turn on the oven light and watch the soufflé rise through the window of the oven door. This creation requires silence. It is pure and good, and therefore, wordless. Do not open the door or the soufflé will fall.

Recipe for global warming:

1 planet
7 continents
5 oceans
400 parts per million of CO_2

It is as easy to crack a planet as to wreck an egg recipe. Putting too much baking powder in its oceans, turning it acidic, cracking its mountains to dig for coal, cooking that coal like a soufflé in an oven, making those broken eggs reach for the clouds, turning the crust golden brown. The temperature rises silently. We yap and yap at it like dogs at the back door, but the carbon is as invisible and as hard of hearing as glass.

Recipe for turtle extinction:

1 female turtle
110 sea turtles
~~One shoreline from where the turtle came~~

We think of eggs as "of the air," or as "union between air and land." They are the material that conjoins the ethereal bird with her terrestrial nest, but eggs also marry marine to terrestrial— or they do for now. As temperatures warm across the globe and glaciers and sea ice continue to melt, the oceans will begin to rise. This is bad news for sea turtles. Sea turtles lay their eggs on the same beaches upon which they were born.

Imagine you are a young female turtle. You were hatched from an egg buried in a nest of sand. You flip-flopped your way to the water, avoiding seagull and tsunami. You spent a year or two spinning around the ocean but then some male turtle swam by and knocked you up. No skin off his nose. He just keeps swimming. But now, in addition to your having to carry these fertilized eggs (as if your shell wasn't heavy enough), something inside you has been triggered and now you must swim in a certain direction, toward a certain beach, to lay these eggs. For the eggs to make it, they need crusty sand, hot air, whipping wind. You arrive at the general vicinity but nothing smells the same. You swim shoreward but instead of finding sand, your legs are still kicking in deep water. Your long-memory flickers: the waters shallow and see-through blue. These waters are still dark. The ocean floor is a Brontosaurus-height below. The part of you that remembers waters is the species memory that remembers brontosauri 165 million species-years ago. You swim around in circles like a dog looking for a place to lie down but you never find that place. The eggs stay inside. The turtle swims on. You have no say in the matter. Turtles have always been quiet creatures. Turtle birth, like egg cooking, is time-dependent. The female turtle can swim and swim and swim but eventually, like all women, her ovaries give out.

Recipe for eggs poached in broth:

There is no recipe. Poach the eggs in broth

I have read religiously the Julia Child recipe for omelets. I have seen Jacques Pépin make omelets with chopsticks. I have beaten eggs in a bowl and poured them into butter in a nonstick pan and moved the eggs around until it seemed I'd never get them flat again. I've rolled the omelet onto itself and then onto a plate, but I have never eaten an omelet so good as the one I made using beef consommé. I've looked and looked for the recipe but I can't find one. I thought beef consommé omelet was a thing but perhaps it is not a thing. Now, what I mostly end up with is something like egg drop soup, which is also delicious because the surface area of the broth matches the surface area of the stomach and the proteins in the egg pin down that immediate, surface satisfaction, with a deeper, more permanent satisfaction.

Sometimes, it's the simplest things that are the hardest. Like riding your bicycle, something most five-year-olds can accomplish. It is as easy as poaching an egg but it does take time and some skill and there are hills and also too-hard-boiling water, but eggs poached in water require no dead chickens and bicycles require no more carbon dioxide than a human naturally breathes out and no more energy than frying an egg, if you poach the egg in a reasonably small amount of water. If only we could eat poached eggs and ride bikes exclusively. Even the chickens, though still in service, would be grateful to keep their heads.

Recipe for poached eggs:

fresh eggs
slightly, but not overly, boiling water

Proportion isn't as easy as it looks. "Slightly boiling" is an ineffable phrase. How many bubbles per square inch? What percentage of the water should boil? When water reaches 212 degrees Fahrenheit does that mean the whole of the water is as hot as it can get, or just the bubbles that you can see?

It is important to ask questions of the water as much as it is to ask questions of the egg. Remember, we're in this together—the chicken notwithstanding.

Science experiments are cooking, too. Remember, dear Generation Xers, we have missed the mark. The temperatures have arisen 2 degrees Celsius—the ceiling temperature increase scientists argue will set off catastrophic climate change. It's up to the Millennials now.

Zoe's science project is due. Zoe, who is going to save the planet with her solar oven, carbon scrubbing device, and slippers she will invent for easier floor mopping, is a fan of the science fair. She wanted to test to see if dogs' saliva killed other bacteria-like bacteria in boogers, mold, and human saliva but (a), we don't have a high-powered microscope, and (b), layering objects with saliva seemed kind of gross, so instead she turned her focus toward an egg shrinking/egg-enlarging project that was awesome since I am immersed in all things egg.

How to shrink an egg:

2 boiled eggs.
vinegar
corn syrup
48 hours.

Soak the hard-boiled shell in vinegar. Overnight, the vinegar will react with the shell, turning the carbon of the shell into carbon dioxide. Watch the vinegar bubble. You will be left with a thick membrane you had no idea existed between the hard carbon shell and the egg white. This is NOT the thin membrane that sticks to a regular, I'm-just-going-to-eat-this hard-boiled egg. Take the now-squeezy egg, its pliability comparable to a stress ball, its resilience probably not so plastic. But it feels so stable.

Immerse one of these stable eggs in water, the other egg in corn syrup.

Overnight, the egg submerged in water expands. The one soaked in corn syrup shrinks. Why does the egg submerged in corn syrup shrink? The membrane is permeable enough to let the smaller-sized water molecules escape from the egg, but the larger-sized sugar molecules cannot get inside. The egg submerged in water allows the water molecules to travel back and forth, leaving that egg about the same size it was to start.

Here's a planet as egg, shrink-wrapped by carbon rather than corn syrup but still losing water, at least the potable, egg-poaching kind, every day. The world gets smaller every year, they say, metaphorically, at Disneyland. No one thought that driving our cars and burning our goal would make it literal. Suffocating. Tight dress on a full stomach. Perhaps we could manufacture a few million more stress balls as the water evaporates, as the aquifer dries up, as the ice shelf melts?

The surface of the planet is 71 percent water; about 96 percent of that water is saline. The planet looks incredibly blue from space, but much of that water is good only for salt-water-living plants and animals. The octopi and the dolphins like it. The rest of us have to spend a lot of money to access potable water, walk a long way to get to the water, or rearrange the riverways, to get the water to come to us. It takes nearly fifty-three gallons of water to produce one egg in the mass-produced-egg industry. Chickens feed on grain that requires a lot of water to grow.

Would raising backyard chickens require as much water? Not if you were efficient about it. When you're rinsing the sprouts you're growing in your Mason jars, you can collect the water you used to soak and rinse them for the chickens to drink. And, although you may need to buy them some grain from the Tractor Supply store sometimes, you can also feed them leftovers. Chickens will eat anything—even chicken soup. The surface area of broth satisfies everyone. Homegrown chickens and solar-powered ovens: Save the planet, one egg at a time.

Scrambled eggs:

Crack them in a bowl. Whisk them.
Add a pinch of salt.
A pinch of pepper.
Put them in a pan. A pan on low heat. I know you're hungry.
Low, though. Low.

Eggs react intensely to the pan. If you put eggs in a too-hot pan their proteins seize up. Heat is more of a killer than motion.

Eggs withstand a good whipping. Harold McGee writes in *On Food and Cooking: The Science and Lore of the Kitchen*, "Scrambled eggs made in the usual quick, offhand way are usually hard and forgettable. The key to moist scrambled eggs is low heat and patience; they will take several minutes to cook."[1] A student, Gary Fish, in one of the first classes I taught as a professor, taught me, "Low and slow, let the pan hug the eggs with heat, but not strangle them." It takes a long time to learn how to teach writing, even longer to learn how to slow down to cook an egg.

Slow cooking is important for the egg. Slow cooking includes nearly everything you do to the egg. When you make custard, you want to add hot ingredients to the cold, putting in hot milk a little at a time to temper the eggs. If you add cold eggs to hot milk, the protein molecules separate from the water molecules and you get clumps of curdled eggs and a stringy liquid mass strewn throughout your would-have-been pudding. It is nearly as impossible to repair a mess of stringy egg as it is to repair a fractured rainforest or revise a pointless story.

But a little heat makes the molecules move around gently. By slow cooking or adding the eggs slowly, you give the protein molecules time to adjust, inviting water molecules to bond with them. At a low, less panicky temperature, the proteins aren't xenophobic; they are friendly, diplomatic. A lot of heat freaks them out. The proteins cling together in fear, not allowing water molecules in. With a lot of heat you get fried eggs that become rubbery and custards that become lumpy and no one is getting along and everyone is hungry.

Recipe for how to make yourself believe everything is going to be all right:

1 pound easy-migration imagination
3 pounds "I've seen polar bears adapt before" refrain
1.5 pounds bikini—who doesn't love warmer temps?
10 pounds strawberries. Everyone can live on strawberries
15 goose eggs to distract the bears that might think ringed seals and human seals taste pretty similar

Slowly. Slowly the planet warms. We can't all move north, at least not quickly. Our xenophobia increases in correlation to time and space. Surely, we could get along if we met each under slower, less panicky circumstances.

Researcher Antero Järvinen from the University of Helsinki studied the effects of global warming on bird eggs.[2] One shouldn't be able to study the effects of global warming on bird eggs over nineteen years. That is too fast for a planet to warm. Adaptation is a slow, generational process. Most of us haven't even had kids by nineteen. When a planet warms, it should do so slowly, over eons. Two degrees Celsius in a human lifetime is a speed of warming that has never been witnessed on earth, unless you count the heat from the events caused by the asteroid that killed the dinosaurs. When you're talking about effects of global warming, you don't want to compare your age to that of the dinosaur extinction—a hard metaphor to live with.

Although Järvinen had only nineteen years to study the eggs, he found some significant changes in the amount of resources the pied flycatcher, a long-distance migrating bird that winters in Africa, devoted to egg growth. He saw increases in egg volume, which "Warm weather during the egg laying period was the probable cause of an increase in egg volume" (109). Although the egg size increased overtime, overall success of the fledglings did not increase, most likely because although overall temperatures increased, cold spells occurred as often. Very cold spells, especially in northern Finland, can kill baby birds quickly. Still, Järvinen concludes that, "some of the results herein supported the hypothesis that global warming may have favourable effects on the reproduction of birds. This in turn may help them rapidly conquer new areas when they become available and compensate for rising mortality rates to be expected elsewhere where warming means desiccation" (110). The point here is that in northern areas, birds may have time to warm their eggs slowly. In the southern regions, eggs may warm too quickly to adapt, cooking the would-be babies inside.[3]

In northern countries, it might seem like a good thing that these eggs will be bigger. Maybe big eggs will save other species. Some climate change optimists have argued that polar bears can adapt their diet from sea-based to land-based.

Goose eggs and berries abound—except, some argue, there are not enough goose eggs in all the land to feed the largest bears on earth. The protein content in an egg isn't the same as in a seal. Ringed seals, the primary diet for polar bears, are 34 percent fat. Goose eggs are also nearly 30 percent fat, and, as noted by Järvinen, northerly eggs are likely to grow bigger due to global warming, but that does not mean there will be enough eggs to feed all the bears. Earth Touch News reports in the article "Climate Change Will Scramble Polar Bears' Diets—and Eggs Aren't the Solution" reports that "Five of the major genetic differences between brown bears and polar bears involve metabolising lipids, which includes fats and fat-soluble vitamins. This means a land-based diet of proteins and carbohydrates may not suit the physical needs of polar bears."[4]

Likely too, the current brown bears in habitats of northern Alaska do what they can to make a living off the land, right next to where the polar bears once thrived, living by the sea. These brown bears are the smallest and least well dispersed of all the brown bears. Now, as the polar bears turn toward their food, competition will abound. The geese have wings. They can leave that cold town, head south, even head north, further away from the hungry bears. Their fat eggs may ensure their own survival but now the bears are left with only berries that, if you check the USDA's Web site for nutrition content, have no fat content whatsoever. All those bears in the north aren't going to make it. I guess the climate change optimists might say that's all right. The humans will need to move there quickly to take over the ground, claim the berries, trap the geese, force them to leave their fat eggs with you.

Recipe for an apocalyptic novel:

1 Viggo Mortensen—as either Aragorn, or the father in Cormac McCarthy's *The Road*.

2 Black and white film, or, barring that, a lot of ash strewn about.

3 A tank or a shopping cart.

4 Hard-boiled eggs. Portable and something you can pawn off on a chicken if you need to blame someone for the apocalypse.

5 Recipes for eggs for the future. Because an apocalypse always ends. Otherwise, they wouldn't make a movie out of your book.

There are a lot of egg recipes. Could you survive on eggs alone? Would your cholesterol get too high? Would you come down with scurvy? What if butter wasn't one of your free ingredients? Still, if you were allotted butter, lemon, flour, and spinach, you might be able to survive, happily, for a number of weeks, on eggs alone. Begin with eggs Benedict (You can make your own English muffins! You can borrow Canadian bacon from the Canadians. They're a sharing people). Spinach salad with hard-boiled eggs for lunch. You can make lemon curd for dessert, spinach soufflé for dinner.

The next day, eggs scrambled in hollandaise sauce leftover from breakfast the day before. Egg salad sandwiches. Quiche for supper. Pancakes for breakfast, deviled eggs for lunch, egg drop soup for dinner. Eggs baked in ham cream with spinach on the side. Spinach covered with béarnaise. Cheesy poofs are easy to make. Make a béchamel (I know. You are forever making béchamel when you're talking to me). Whip an egg into the béchamel; wait until it's completely incorporated, whip in another. Add gruyère. Dollop onto sheet pan. Bake for 425 minutes. Cheesy cream puffs: a homemade, noncrunchy Cheeto. The apocalypse with cheese and eggs. If you can cook (and have access to cheese) maybe you will be the one to survive.

Funeral potatoes:

1 package hash browns
1 can Campbell's mushroom soup
1 can fried onions
There are no eggs in this recipe but if it is the end of the world/your funeral, you want nonperishable items anyway.

Every Mormon funeral boasts funeral potatoes served in the gym of the neighborhood ward house. I grew up with the end of the world. Mormon church. Wasatch Fault. Father's drinking. It lets me pretend I'm able to take these things in stride. The end of the bird. The end of the world. It's a tiny shaking, these minor household dramas. The glaciers that made the Little and Big Cottonwood canyons, those were big things. The earthquake they promise will liquefy the Salt Lake Valley and pull down the fancy houses on the foothills— that's a big thing. They have predicted that two tectonic plates in the bottom of the Pacific Ocean haven't released enough tension, that they're saving it up for the big one—a tsunami that could drown California. Small things include the white bird with black wings that has gone extinct. The goose that laid the golden egg was, after the hunter killed her, found to be just a regular, non-gold-on-the-inside goose. In this case, it's not what was literally inside the goose that counted; it was what the insides could make. The goose was an artist. Never kill the artists to scoop out the art, leave them alive but oppressed—they'll make millions of tiny, ornate metaphors for you. Now there are no more golden eggs, no more golden geese, no more passenger pigeons. Big and little apocalypses threaten every day.

As the living goose and living artist know, there is always a chance for revision. Once upon a time, bald eagles nearly went extinct. Then a clever ban on the pesticide DDT put an end to thin-shelled bald eagle eggs. The bald eagles may not think their whole world is restored—they have to sit on man-made telephone poles rather than snags. They dodge cars. They eat lead-filled bullets and die of lead poisoning like the much-less-well-off condors. But it is no small thing that the birds of which there were only seventy-six pairs left in the world have rebounded to numbers too big to count. Maybe there are no small things. Maybe the beginning of order is to count all the small things—each ant, each tree, each bird, each egg—to see how large things can be.

You would think that if humans can figure out how, with eggs, to puff a soufflé, make meringues and divinity, balloon pâte choux, glue flour and sugar into cookies, surely you can undo this global warming. You don't need to know the exact science of how custard sets to set custard; you just need to get the proportion right. Eggs are excellent because they increase their surface area as you cook with them. Only a few other things do that: yeast for bread, baking powder and baking soda for cakes and cookies. Usually, cooking shrinks things but as there are more people on the planet who require more arable land and more potable water, a bigger planet is what we need. We need to think like an egg: add proper ingredients, the right amount of heat. We need patience and quiet footing. Don't stomp on the ground outside the oven. Let the soufflé rise.

Spoons

You shove so much personal loss into the giant shell of world problems. You allow your personal sadnesses to balloon like globes. Which came first: the fear of the end or the fear of the beginning? The worry over the apocalypse or the worry that your world would never get started? It would be nice, you imagine, to carry all your worries in the space of an egg. It fits in your hand. If it fits in your hand, you can take care of it. If it fits in your hand, you can keep the worries from always coming true.

That game—the one where you run to the end of the row with a spoon holding an egg and you try not to drop that egg? It's the transfer that's the hard part. Communicating that egg into the welcoming bowl of your teammate's spoon. It's hard to say. Have you put all these dreams into one basket? Are your hopes and dreams for the future just a dream that the future keeps going? Back and forth we pass this little egg. Charged with spoons, humans will parent anything.

The glue that holds us together

It was the worst thing that could have spilled. I'd needed the yolks for something: egg wash? Soufflé? Avgolemono? Perhaps cheesy poofs? So I saved the egg whites as one does when one thinks one makes more meringues or more "healthy" omelets than one will ever make. They sat on the back shelf in a Tupperware for a long time. Long enough for me to forget what I'd used their yolky counterpart for.

I was pulling tortillas from the lower shelf when I noticed; I could not *not* notice because the package of tortillas would not budge. I pulled and pulled and merely ripped the plastic. The tortillas were stuck. I took them out one by one, leaving the plastic until morning.

The whites had spilled everywhere. The Tupperware betrayed me. The white glued not only the tortilla package to the shelves, but also the glass shelf insert to the plastic shelf holder. To pull the shelf out, I had to scrape and soak, scrape and soak. Each drawer needed to be removed. Sour cream and yogurt containers bound permanently to each other had to be thrown away. Blue craters of sponge tore and stuck. I needed a knife. I needed a chisel. I needed to promise myself I would freeze egg whites or chuck them from now on.

Kids chucked eggs at my in-laws' house. When I told Rick about my egg white problem, he said, "There is nothing worse." He had to take a steel brush to his concrete. An egg, pitched at a window, had made a sieve of his screen. More brushing. More scrubbing.

●

What a waste, I thought, all that scrubbing. We could have repainted a porch, built a patio, done all the laundry in the time it took to undo what the eggs and some temperamental Tupperware/teenagers had done. And what of the eggs? The eggs thrown were most likely not from cage-free hens. Wasted chicken lives. Wasted calories. Wasted protein all around and yet a good reminder that—if and when everything has gone to waste—eggs make an excellent glue, at least if it never rains.

All the eggs in Israel

It is a lonely adventure, cooking eggs all alone. I'm in my kitchen. I look over my shoulder as I wet my finger, drag a wayward shell from the bowl holding the egg. Should I make one or two? Sixty calories. I have no cream. No ham. No friend over for lunch. Kids are at school. Erik is at work. I have grading to do. I should finish that book review. Fine-tune the essay.

And yet, I want something more than scrambled or poached eggs. I want something with a crust, some melty cheese. But I don't want to make a soufflé. I settle for a quick frittata even though the edges tend to get a little rubbery and all I have for stuffing is leftover broccoli. I add too much cheese. I burn the bottom. As I try to flip the eggy pancake, I miss, it half slops out of the pan. The other half, I have to fold over with my hand.

No one is watching so I scoop the spilled eggs from under the burner and add them to the others. I tap on the top of the frittata with a spatula saying to myself, "Nothing to see here. Nothing to see."

No one is listening because no one is here. If Erik had been home, he would have flipped the frittata for me. If Rebecca had been over, she would have held a plate alongside the pan so I could slide the frittata onto it and flip it over. She would have told me how her mother made egg stuff and how it's easier than a frittata but there is no way you would make egg stuff for one.

If one of the ways one tries to understand the world is through the things of the world, then my messy frittata is my messy story. If I ask my mom about when I first started cooking, she'll tell the story of how I made tacos for the whole family when I was eight. When I show her my novel about a little girl who cooks an egg at age four, she'll shake her head and say that's impossible. A story made by one person is a bit of a messy frittata, a fallen soufflé. A story made by many is rich and multilayered, soaked in milk overnight, cooked solid so you could poke it with a stick and it wouldn't collapse under its own weight.

Sometimes, you get sick of your own story. Sometimes, you get sick of your own idioms. I am tired of knowing that I have to crack a few eggs to make an omelet. I want to know what to do with the shells. A creation myth is pretty lonely if you only write it about yourself. The creation myth is supposed to tell you the story of a whole world, an entire people. I want to make this story something more than my own. So I bug people for their egg stories. And they, in turn, bug their families. Egg strata by petition or coercion.

🥚

My friend Margot Singer wrote a novel called "Underground Fugue," about a Jewish woman, Esther, whose son has died, drowned when he was fourteen in a river. Esther goes through the motions, tries to get her life on track. But she cannot get her life on track. She and her husband divorce. She moves to London to help her mother who is dying—to help her die. 9/11 looms in the background. So does the holocaust. She plays fugues on the piano. Death is everywhere. The next-door neighbor's son might be up to no good. He might be up to all kinds of good but in this book, this Jewish woman imagines the worst about her Muslim neighbor. She imagines the best. She falls in love with the father of this maybe-up-to-no-good boy. But, because her imagination is as wall-y as the wall between Palestine and Israel, between East Germany and West, between the Ghetto and Krakow, the father and the woman cannot get on track together. Her mother dies. Esther leaves London. The father and the son stay on doing as much good as they can.

A few years ago, Margot approached me about putting together a series of panels to be hosted at the Association of Writers & Writing Programs (AWP) writing conference. She thought we could do something similar. We balance each other well. She is smart, methodical, organized, had a previous career as a consultant on Wall Street and is an extremely vivid, precise, worldly writer. And I am not only "effervescent," but also have strong opinions about nonfiction and hybridity. I argue strongly and often enough that hybrid writing is good writing, that together we have convinced at least twelve people, including the editors who published *Bending Genre*, our eventual book about creative nonfiction, that we are right. A "we" is so much better than an "I" in these things.

When I see Margot, she always tells me excellent stories about her dad and how he's not sure why she doesn't visit him more and why she left her consulting career to become a writer. She tries to explain to him she has one of the best jobs in the land at Denison University. She tries to tell him writing is important. Think of the books written about Auschwitz, she reminds him. She and I talk about how Primo Levi, in his book *The Periodic Table,* uses elements from the periodic table as catalysts for memory and story. She wrote about this in Essay Daily, "Levi invented a new genre, a hybrid of science and literature, a blend of essay, allegory, fiction, memoir." The importance of memory and memoir was important to Levi. His book, *Survival in Auschwitz,* documents that how he survived was in part due to how he remembered. Levi does die. Some think he killed himself by throwing himself down the stairs. Margot tells us that, "No one knows exactly what happened in that stairwell, on that day, but we do know that Levi worried that the lessons of the Holocaust would be forgotten, and struggled terribly with the burden of remembering and bearing witness to the past." A memory is individually important to its rememberer. I reach for that whole egg but it rolls and tumbles out of my brain. I catch a glimpse but even in so catching, it shatters. I am alone, chasing that memory. It's the struggle for memory that unites us. We are all always trying to remember that story. To put that broken egg back together. For *Bending*

Genre, Margot and I collected essays about various kinds of nonfiction writing, but almost all nonfiction has some bearing on generation of memory. How is memory created? How is it destroyed? Where do we get the stuff from which to write? Levi took the Periodic Table. He took Auschwitz. Margot took her Jewish heritage, the anti-Muslim sentiment that followed 9/11. I take mistakes I make, like leaving the eggs on the counter, which you cannot do in this country, and turned them into a salmonella story.

Some people do not want to make stories. When I asked Margot for her dad's egg story, she said, "It was like pulling teeth to get these stories. All my dad would say was, 'I remember my mother taking boiled eggs, taking the yellow yolk out, mixing it together with onion and paprika, and putting it back into the white shell. . . . I think she called them "Devil's eggs."'" (We then decided it must have been Gefultte Eier (stuffed eggs) in German.) I also got this from him:

My father had a soft-boiled egg for breakfast every morning.

My mother said: "I had to make supper for my little brother, from the time when I was about eleven or twelve. Usually I made scrambled eggs. We had a small bowl and I had to beat the eggs with a fork quickly and without spilling. Once I mastered it, I thought to myself, 'I'm going to be a good cook!' I felt very proud of myself."

Margot tells me in an email, "My mother doesn't add that her mother passed away when she was thirteen and presumably was very sick at this time. She was born in 1934, so she is talking about around 1945 to 1946."

Margot's mom grew up in Portland, Maine. Her father the doctor emigrated from Lithuania in the mid-1930s.

My father was born in Czechoslovakia but emigrated to Palestine (Israel) in 1939 when he was nine years old, so the egg memory surely comes from Israel. (I remember my grandmother's stuffed eggs too. She always put them in little cupcake papers.)

My grandmother's friend, Anny Stern, left Czechoslovakia for Palestine, but her mother, Mina Pächter, was sent to Theriesienstadt (Terezín). The starving and undernourished women in the camp put together a handwritten cookbook. In the fall of 1944, Mina entrusted the cookbook to a friend, asking that if he survived he give it to her daughter Anny in Palestine. He did survive but had no way of finding Anny. Somehow, twenty-five years later, the package finally found its way to Anny, who was then living in New York City. I knew Anny when I lived in New York in the late 1980s/early 1990s (I used to go to visit her quite often, and we would swim in the swimming pool on the roof of her building in the East 20s. We'd also go to New York Philharmonic concerts together at Lincoln Center—she had fabulous tickets.), and she told me the story. The cookbook, *In Memory's Kitchen*, was published around that same time, not long before she died.[1]

This is the recipe Margot remembers as "Packed and Filled Eggs."

Pächter and gefüllte:
Hard boil 10 eggs, cut them in half. Remove yolks and press them through a sieve. Add 5 decagrams butter, 2 anchovies pressed through a sieve, a little mustard, 3–4 drops Maggi [liquid seasoning]; ⅛ liter whipped heavy cream, parsley, lemon juice. Now put eggs on a platter. Pour [liquid] aspic over. Before [pouring on the aspic] let fantasy run free and the eggs are garnished with ham, [smoked] salmon, caviar, capers. One can put the eggs into paper cuffs and serve them with hot sliced rolls.

This recipe is so similar to one for deviled eggs but one step over, to the left. The cultures cross without mayonnaise but with mustard. If egg is the memory, the stuffing is the story and Margot brings me her parents' story through the story of this rescued recipe in a rescued cookbook across borders and countries and through anti-Semitism and anti-Muslim sentiments and across boundaries of nonfiction and fiction and hybridity to say, Here, I give you this egg. It's unfamiliar in its paper cuff but in your mouth you will remember the taste.

All the eggs in Ukraine

I met Tanya when I was hired to be the Administrative Assistant at the Oregon Winegrowers Association. Hired at $19,500 a year. I was a bargain to the organization. It was a lot of money to me, though. The house I lived in cost $600 a month and I had two roommates. My car was old but paid off. Living in Portland cost less then than it does now. I had only to buy beer and grilled cheese at Dots. I liked the job because it tangentially related to my English degree. I wrote newsletters and brochures. However, unlike being an English major, I had to be there from eight to five. I did not like being there from eight to five. It felt like a prison. I spent more time at the office than at home. I had only eight vacation days. I bugged my boss to allow me to leave early or to run errands or to go to meetings that weren't in the building.

Although the office was housed in the remodeled Alber's Mill, brick washed sallow by Portland's rain, the interior was still all fluorescent lights and industrial carpet. I tried to explain to my boss, Bill, how unnatural it was to be stuck inside all day. I jumped up on the short filing cabinet and yelled "Workers Unite. You have nothing to lose but your chains," but the only other workers there was Doreen, who spent a lot of time on the phone with her husband, and Tanya. Tanya, whose father had escaped the Ukraine before the Iron Curtain fell, didn't think my Marx and Engels reference was that funny. She knew the bad of communism. She was a Republican. She gave tons of money to the homeless shelter. She believed in private, not government, assistance. She said she gave so much because she could picture herself homeless. "I have a vision of myself, complete with shopping cart, rolling my bags down the street. It could happen to any of us." I once attributed that fear to the fear her father must have had, leaving behind all monetary security when he fled the Ukraine but the older I get, the more I understand. It's one small step to the left for any of us. An injury. A move away from New York, a move to New York. A stock slide. An economy crumble. A Soviet-like Stasi that claims you're an insurgent. A Nazi-like SS that pulls you out of your home and sends you to the ghetto, that sends you to Auschwitz like someone's father you once knew.

Like Margot, Tanya had gone to Harvard. She too had worked in New York City as a consultant. And, like Margot, Tanya had quit that lucrative job. In Margot's case, she quit to go to graduate school. Tanya quit the job to move to Portland to be closer to her dad, who was eighty, and her sister Helen. She and Helen planned to buy a hazelnut farm so, to bide her time and save her money, she took odd jobs, working part time at the Oregon Winegrowers Association. Even though I was the English major, Tanya was the experienced writer. She proofread the newsletter I wrote, refining sentences, finding logical inconsistencies. While Bill told me, "The devil is in the details" while he circled my typos, Tanya showed me how to re see the whole story. "If you're writing about the Sokol Blosser Windery, don't forget to include how Susan Sokol and Bill Blosser graduated from Reed College. Since you know Reed and you know they know Reed, the story will mean that much more to you." Tanya might have been my first teacher about personal essay writing. If you make it a little about you, your prose style won't sound like you're pressing hard-boiled eggs through a sieve.

I haven't worked with Tanya in almost twenty years. I left the Winegrowers for the Oregon Humane Society and then for graduate school. She left to start the Pea and Lentil Association. She now lives near Moscow, Idaho, where she has land where she still might start the hazelnut farm, but for now does small jobs for nonprofits, inspiring the newcomer would-be Marxists to write a little bit about themselves, and, when she can, write a little bit of her own story:

When Nicole asked if I could tell her something about Ukrainian Easter eggs, Pysanky, I immediately heard a scratch, scratch, scratch, tap, tap in my mind's ear and I pictured the symbolic, colorful, intricately etched ovals that so many associate with my father's people. The word Pysanky comes from pysaty, meaning "to write" and I believe the pysanky truly does "write" Ukrainian history. It seems of all traditions and traits of this people, the word "eggs" flows like melting wax from the word "Ukrainian" in nearly every nonpolitical mind.

When I think of childhood Easters, I immediately hear the persistent "scratch, scratch, scratch" of the pin my father attached to a whittled stick he used to dip into paraffin that he melted in a jar lid, on top the stove. Then drop by drop he applied the melted wax to paint the pictures and designs from his heart. Dip, scratch, dip, scratch . . . . It took him the full two hours we dyed our three dozen eggs (one each) and then some to complete 4 personalized eggs. After finishing each egg, he would place it carefully into the cup of dye containing each of our favorite colors: blue for my mom, green for Ebet, red for Helen and yellow for me. And on Easter morning, our egg from Tato was the "sign" indicating which Easter basket belonged to whom.

There was consistency to his pin strokes. The "swoosh" always ended with a thick bead and there were often dots and short swirls around the midline. The lines were usually diagonal and rarely met. There was almost always a flower-like figure on one end. The eggs were similar, but never the same. What I never really understood was why *my* Tato's eggs didn't look like the ones in the most common picture books and magazines.

During the summer after my first year of college, I found out. A friend and I ventured to *the* city. She was offered a position with a corporate bank, prepping for her successful career. I found one, then another, then finally a third, perfect job to more than fill my days. I had to be up before 5 each morning to stand at the counter of H & H Bagels East. At 11, I rushed back to our cockroach-inhabited apartment to change clothes so that I could join in a course at the Harness Center Dance Academy. Then two afternoons a week, several evenings and a few weekends, I pursued my heritage.

The Ukrainian Museum recognized my interest and snapped up my eagerness to learn. They even gave me a small wage to classify their entire Ukrainian egg collection. It took me about 15 minutes to realize this would be no easy task. Each pattern and design heralds back to a specific region and sometimes a specific time or influence in history. The styles and colors of neighboring subcultures sometimes spilled across unmarked borders to make it all the more confusing. Each color, picture, graphic and design has special meaning. I didn't just learn about native art, but soon could recognize the various regions and peoples and even histories of the mottled Ukrainian folk.

Now I knew why my Tato's eggs weren't like the ones pictured in the books. His region and his character were smaller, less well known, humbler and gentler (less colorful) than most of the others.

Every year after that summer I appreciated his creations even more. As he dipped and painted and scratched through the years, we watched his hands grow more gnarled and his joints more swollen. When the stylus got too shaky, the patterns changed too. And about the time he gave up his wood carving, my Tato also started using oil paints instead of wax, and wooden eggs instead of fresh ones, to preserve his memories. At the time, it made us sad to see the change and the end of a family tradition, but today I am forever grateful to have eggs that will never crack and that will always carry on the love and affection from his homeland to his grandchildren.

The other sound I hear when I think of Ukrainian Easter eggs is "tap, tap, tap." This comes from the stories Tato told and a tradition we still carry on during Easter breakfast. Before eating a bite, we would each choose one colored egg. Tato would turn to his right, gently holding his egg up to the person beside him. "Tap, tap, tap." Usually it was my little sister, Helen, who pertly held hers up next to his. Whichever eggshell cracked first was out of play. The victor (in the old country, when food was scarce, would get to keep and eat the cracked egg) took his unbroken egg and continued to the next person at the table. This went on until everyone had "tapped eggs" and only one was left whole. That egg, my Tato would ceremoniously peel and cut into pieces numbering that of the people at our table. He would place these on a plate and offer one piece to each member.

Tanya and I keep in touch. She came to my wedding even though I totally fucked up the invitation and neglected to enclose the slip to invite her to the wedding proper, only inviting her to the reception. Tanya and her then-husband Alan gave Erik and me a Patagonia blanket for our wedding. I washed it. It shrunk. But still I keep it in the family room. It's still big enough for legs and toes. I should never be the one to carefully categorize eggs of distinct regions. I would miss the nuance. Probably break the egg. Tanya wrote that she and Bill were getting together. I missed the reunion so I do not know if Bill is still rollerblading or still bearing with young administrative assistants who jump on top of filing cabinets quoting Marx. I do know that Tanya was happy to get my email asking for egg stories. She sent me these stories and lists about eggplants. She reminded me about how a killdeer, a kind of plover who nests her eggs nearly out in the open among rocks, gravel, or cinders, keeps predators from her nest by faking a broken wing, luring the would-be egg snatcher away. Tanya said, "Send me more writing prompts." I sent her a prompt to write a braided essay. I gave her a prompt I give my students: Set a timer. Write for 5 minutes about something that happened to you once for 5 minutes, like the time you and your sister visited Poland and the host family had you over for egg liquor and they couldn't open the egg liquor without the excuse of guests and so convinced you to stay for bottle after bottle as you sipped and sipped, waiting until it seemed polite to go, which it never did. When the timer goes off, write something informational that you know about. Like peas or lentils or the Ukraine or the eggplants you spent years trying to convince people other than the Chinese and Italians that eggplants taste good. When those 5 minutes are up, return to the story about egg liquor and how two men invited you to what you thought were more drinks but, when you translated their inducements, you understood the words "green card marriage" and you and Helen went back to your hotel room, tipsy from egg liquor, alone.

All the eggs in Korea

One of my best friends at the university where I teach is Okim Kang. She and I started teaching for the English Department the same year. We each have two kids, older girls, younger boys, who are also good friends. She's in the linguistics area so she's more like a scientist and has better luck with research funding than I do. Also, she laughs a little at me when I tell her the name of my book. "Quench Your Thirst with Salt? You can't do that. You'll get sick." She's a bit of a literalist. She also knows about salt. And thirst. And sushi. She and her husband, Jinhee, are the best cooks I know. They make pancakes of eggs, mung beans, and scallions. She cooks chicken soup with rice cakes, sliced beef with garlic, fishcakes which look a lot like noodles, her own kimchi, her own sushi. Every time she sees me, she gives me roasted nori, which she imports directly from Korea because the kind here is "too thick and too salty." Not quenching at all.

I see Okim twice a week at the Martial Arts studio where she punches me in the shoulder even though she's not the one taking taekwondo classes.

"Hey, you going to sign the kids up for parents' night out?"

Okim punches me in the arm again. I'm used to it. I kind of like it. She only punches her good friends.

"You have to sign them up. My kids won't go if yours don't."

"I don't really need a babysitter. You know, Erik's mom will watch the kids. I don't even know where we'd go. I am tired of the restaurants in Flagstaff."

But then I see her face fall. She likes that our kids are friends and wants them to hang out.

"OK. I'll sign them up." It's Valentine's Day. Erik and I should do something romantic like take his parents out to dinner. Also, I like to make Okim happy. I like her and the way that she roasts seaweed just for me.

I also admire her work ethic. She gets big grants. She's a big deal in the linguistic world. She pushes her kids. She makes friends by feeding strangers well. I feel like I'm like her, one exponent removed. When I asked her for some Korean proverbs, she sent me these—each one's cautionary tale is about failure or deprivation or loss. No wonder Okim cooks so abundantly:

Hit rock with an egg.—This means, when you try something incomparable, easily being defeated, or trying to do something that is obvious to failure, we say it's almost like hitting rock with an egg.

Can a boiled egg become a chick? Or, *Can a boiled egg hatch a chick*?—When we refer to something which is impossible to happen.

Don't keep all your eggs in one basket.—We have the same one.

A chicken can hatch an egg once it's fed.—If you want anything, you have to invest; unless you make an effort, you can't get any profit.

"About suffering, they were never wrong," says Auden. These proverbs are about failure and triumph, creation and destruction, gaining and losing. We will do anything to make something out of almost nothing. From the stringy substance of an egg small enough to hold in our hand, we will add air and milk and make a soufflé as big as our heads. Can a boiled egg become a chick? No. But you can make a devil out of that boiled egg.

Okim's mom died when she was young. My mom grew up in Evanston, Wyoming. She lived with her mother and grandmother in houses with dirt floors. They got cheese from the Mormon welfare square. My mom's grandpa regularly beat her grandma. Her dad left her mom when she was five, spent most of that time in Huntington, Texas, in jail, he was killed by police when my mom was twelve. Alcoholism and child abuse and sex abuse proliferated. Eggs from the Mormon welfare station helped to keep misery away. I try to write about my grandparents and that scarcity but can't quite access it through the haze of my comfortable life. I do not know where I would go if I needed cheese at a discount. I try to keep an over-abundant amount of cheese in the house, just in case. Okim, who looks into the deep structure of language to apply what she knows about linguistics to how to communicate better, punches instead of speaks sometimes. She understands that words can only do so much.

Okim's mom died when she was very young. She lived with her dad but he worked all day. She had several brothers and sisters but they were all much older. She spent most of her empty days teaching herself to cook. Okim fills her days. She fills her friends' stomachs. She fills her kids brains and bodies. Full, full, full. She will stave off scarcity. She tells me that she remembers eggs when she was growing up in Korea:

"We have a streamed egg pudding. It's not a dessert, though. You basically put egg in water with some seasoning and stream it. Use this food when people have no appetite or have a sensitive stomach." It sounds like a kind of egg drop soup, but without the broth. I don't tell her this because interrupting might stem the flow of stories. I want this book to be filled with her stories as full as her days.

She adds, "Oh, eggs have been precious food traditionally in Korea, not any more though. So they made a soy sauce marinated egg for winter, which is a good source of protein. Also, when people travel, they used to pack boiled eggs, but not any more, I think."

Okim, who hasn't been back to Korea but once in fifteen years, who received her PhD from Georgia, who ended up in, of all places, Flagstaff, Arizona—where we just got our first Korean restaurant which is too expensive for either me or Okim to visit very often—seems like the kind of person who would take a hard-boiled egg wherever she goes. Who knows when she will get home again and Flagstaff is a high desert mountain town. We could run out of water, run out of supplies, run out of eggs at any minute, but probably not out of stories, punctuated by arm punches.

All the eggs in China

Who will tell us what? Almost anyone, it turns out, if you ask about eggs. I would like to ask our Chinese scholars if they considered bringing hard-boiled eggs with them to the United States. In my department, English faculty mentor visiting scholars, which I think means taking them to coffee and dinner and inviting them to Thanksgiving. How could I pass up asking visitors so proximate to me, who had come from so far away, what their experience with eggs was? To me, the fact that they who are just learning English, who know Mandarin and at least one other Chinese language, were willing to write me their egg stories, became a kind of mentor to me. In relaying these stories, I wondered whether I should "correct" their English. I think it would be condescending to change their words. Think about it this way: Do I know Chinese? I do not. So instead of editing and revising their words, I imagine these gifts as hard-boiled, perfect egg stories shuttled all the way from Beijing by brave scholars who were kind enough to write these stories for me in a language that I know.

When I was twelve my mother gave me a collection of poems, *Women Poets of China*. I remember the white cover, the white space around their words. I remember the way they sent men off to war. The way they worked the fields. I remember a peach, maybe some bread. I still have this book but it's at my office so I rely only on my memory, but I do know that I remember reading and thinking that if I ever go to China, then I would be a real writer like these women.

The women scholars who replied to me want to be writers. What does it mean to want to write in China? Do you have to have a real job first—be a professor or a bartender? As Chinese rural population relocates to the cities, will they write about fire hydrants and sidewalks? Plum trees growing through concrete? The nice thing about eggs, they are rural and urban, farmstead and apartment, inland and oceanfront, Eastern and Western. The egg translates; do stories of the egg? Their willingness to share them makes me think so. Their willingness to translate their stories about their mothers, their idiom, their recipes into English just because I sent them an email make them the most generous and gifted writers I know.

Wiehong Wang

My knowledge about eggs: Eggs play an important part in Chinese people's lives. In my memory, my mother always boil one egg for me on my birthday, as eggs imply "completeness, perfection" in my culture this implication comes from its shape, round has the similar pronunciation as completeness.

When a new baby was born, relatives, friends, and neighbors all bring eggs to the family to show their congratulation. Eggs are the main source of nutrition for the new mother to get recovered from labor.

Besides boiling, steaming or frying, our people have special ways of cooking eggs. Some special ways of eating eggs:

1   Preserved egg (pine-flower eggs)
    How to make it: to put raw eggs into lime—water, then wrap them with chaff.
2   Tea egg
    How to make it: To boil eggx in the tea and other spice.
3   Unhatched eggs In southern part of China, some people eat unhatched, ferttilized eggs. This tradition comes from ancient time when people were very poor and had little to eat. I personally disgust this eating.

Some idioms about eggs:

1   jī dàn lāo gu tou tia
    Literal meaning: try to pick out bones from eggs.
    Meaning: very picky, fastidious.
2   cāng yíng bù bào méi féng de dàn
    Literal meaning: Flies go for cracked eggs Meaning: evil people or influence corrupt only those who have weakness.
3   yi daàn peèng shí
    Literal meaning: to strike an egg against stone. Meaning: being over-confident, work one's own ruin.

4 jī fēi dàn da
Literal meaning: the chicken flies away while the eggs in the coop are broke. Meaning: all is lost, dead loss.

5 shā jī qu dàn Literal meaning: kill the chicken to take out the eggs. Meaning: to kill the golden goose, being short-sighted.

6 xi dàn
Meaning: red painted eggs, presented to friends on the third day of the birth of one's baby.

I learn new words from retyping Wiehong's story: I believe *dàn* means egg. I would also like to use the phrase "Like flies to a cracked egg" more often. Also, when my daughter Zoe eats, she picks bones from chicken. She loves trout but only with three-butter sauce. She loves bananas but only if they're still slightly green. She likes bratwurst but no bun. And flies do go for cracked eggs. Gossip works like this. Find someone who turned their eyes away from their kid for 1 second and something bad, like falling into a gorilla enclosure, and the world piles on. Eggs make the best idioms across the lands. Clichés that are little nuggets of history, literal meanings, moral meanings, stories as an egg yolk, translators crack the shell. Also, I have learned I am prone to typos and misstatements, as I go over the pieces I wrote in what is supposedly my native language, where I am supposedly good at putting sentences together. English is hard, even for native speakers. How brave that Wiehong would send me her story. How lucky I am to hold it in my hand.

Hui Lang—The story of egg:

When I was very young, to me, egg means the love of mother. Especially when I have no appetite or I am ill, mum will cook a bole of Chinese noodles with a poached egg. This can satisfy every child's dream.

In spring Festival, every family will make some delicious foods using eggs, for example, egg roll. This is the favorite food of my father. Every year, he makes a lot to us. Outside there is a slice of egg, but inside will be the meat paste, usually the pork paste, with some dressing. Now it is still our traditional food.

With the age increasing, eggs are put into more elements. In the Tomb-sweeping day (one of our traditional festival), in some places, they have the game called "egg hunts," which is very interesting, especially for children. It is just like the "trick or treating" in Halloween. Another important custom in the very day will be boiling eggs with Artemisia argyi or felon herb. It is said to prevent illness.

The function of egg is very wide. One of the practices in my family is to use it as the fertilizer for the flowers. It is so smelly that we almost fall down. However, my mum especially prefers this peculiar way. Just imagine in the hottest summer, the power of smelly feeling is absolutely strong. We could accept this method when looking at the flourishing plants in our little garden.

We have a lot of good memories about eggs. I hope you like to read my story.

The egg, stretchy, elastic, gluey, sticky thing that it is pulls the memory of the mother. "Egg means love of mother." She fed scrambled eggs first—not a lot. She made you cakes and cookies, pancakes and noodles. Your life is a pyramid with a solid base made out of egg your mother poured. She'll remind you how she fed you. You will write a story about her to repay her. She might not like it but then, you didn't necessarily like eggs at first either.

Hailing Lu

Dear Nicole,

Yes, I'm interested in egg stories and I'd like very much to share with you. Writing is never a burden to me. I like sharing with friends my ideas and thinking.

I like creative writing very much. To name two favorite writers, Peter Hessler and Bill Bryson. They are popular in China. Hessler's book "River Town" is very well-received in China. Some of my students love it very much and one of them has chosen the translations of the book as the research subject of her graduation thesis. Almost all of Bryson's books have been translated into Chinese. I like his sense of humor. As I wander in Barnes&Noble and Bookmans, I often marvel at the creativity of American writers. I came across an interesting book entitled *The Writing Diet—Write Your Right Size*, It presents a brilliant plan for using one of the soul's deepest and most abiding appetites—the desire to be creative—to lose weight and keep it off forever. I wonder if your works are available on the Internet and I'd like very much to read your writings.

Here are my stories of eggs and some traditions of eggs:

Egg Stories of My Generation

I hated hard-boiled eggs when I was a little girl. But my mother always gave my one hard-boiled egg at breakfast every morning before school. She said it was for nutrition and I must eat it. Sometimes I ate the egg white (I found easier to swallow) and hid the yolk (nasty and hard to swallow) under the table and fled to school. Of course I'd be scolded when I came back home after school. Eggs were expensive at that time (in the 1970s) in China and often used as gifts when visiting friends and relatives. My mother had good reason to be mad at me.

Interestingly, my husband had similar stories when he was young. He hid egg yolk in a trash can behind a door. His mother found it and washed the yolk and ate it. I guess a lot of Chinese of my age had similar experiences. Parents saved eggs for their kids while kids were too young to understand their love.

A friend of mine told me his story of eggs which I find so amusing that I'd like to share with you. He grew up in a poor farmers' family. There were four kids in the family and life was hard for them. His parents had some hens in the yard and eggs were collected every day and stored in a basket hung very high above from the ceiling to avoid rats. In the countryside at that time eggs were rarely eaten as they were often used to trade salt, sauces or other commodities when vendors came to the village or sold on a farmer's market for cash. Eggs meant money to farmers. Egg-laying hens were called "Farmer's Bank". Scrambled eggs were a special dish for guests, so only when there was a guest in the family could the kids have the chance to eat. The smart kid, my friend one day was trying to steal an egg from the basket but found it too high and that could be detected by his parents as eggs were counted every day. Then an idea came to him as one hen just laid an egg and he grabbed it and as he was excited thinking where and how he could have it cooked he heard footsteps of his parents coming back home. He immediately put the egg in his pocket but unluckily the egg was broken and the liquid of raw white and yolk trickling down his pants to his feet. What a funny picture! He said, "I still remember the sticky coolness of that broken egg on my leg." We both laughed heartily at this point of his story and yet I know for a little boy it wasn't funny at all at the time.

For school kids there was a superstitious fad that if you eat two eggs at breakfast before the exam, you'll get good luck. Two eggs stands for the double zeroes of 100 (the highest score in our system of grades).

There are many customs of eggs in China. In my view, the most well-known one is "red eggs". It's been a long tradition that families with newly-born babies will give "red eggs" to relatives, friends and neighbors. Red eggs are hard boiled eggs with red-dyed shells. The color red symbolizes fortune, luck and happiness in Chinese culture. Strangers will get red eggs too when they pass by the house as the family would like to share happiness and good luck.

We have "colorful eggs" for a well-known festival—the Dragon Boat Festival. I wonder if you have heard of this. It is to commemorate a patriotic poet, named Quyuan, who drowned himself when he found hopeless to save his country and his king. Besides, Zongzi, a traditional food for the festival, kids will get colored eggs on the festival. They can take eggs to school and have a game of "bumping eggs" with friends. In the game, each kid holds one egg in hand and crashes the egg with another. If the egg gets cracked or smashed, the owner is out. The kid who has the hardest egg wins the game. Kids have great fun in the game and eat the cracked eggs together.

So far that's what have come to my mind as I write this email. Hope it can be useful to you. I can write more to you tomorrow morning if you need. My roommates and I'll be busy cooking in the afternoon as we have some guests visiting our dorm tonight.

Keep in touch.

I hope they are making eggs in their dorm room even if Hailing doesn't love eggs. I hope that she, after writing this, thought that writing was even more fun. I hope that she becomes China's Peter Hessler, translating the US for Chinese readers. I hope that she plays crashing eggs with her dormmates. I hope that she knows how lucky I am for this gift. I hope she tells this story again. Eggs are lucky indeed, written and read, as brightly as the color red.

Eggs in Utah

Rebecca had been in the hospital for a week with her oldest child when I called to ask her about eggs. She's exhausted and behind at work and in between two gallery openings, one of them entitled *You Are Here*, portraits showcasing nineteen female artists in an art world where 70 percent of the gallery exhibitors are male. Her son is still on oxygen for bronchitis. "But I wanted to tell you my egg stories," she said. "I have two. The first one is that when we were kids, Easter wasn't the same. I don't know if it was because I was the youngest of seven or times were just different then. My mom would give us Easter Baskets. We would keep the baskets all year long. With my kids, I throw like 90% of the candy away we get for holidays. Not my mom. Sometimes, she'd hide the Easter baskets on the heater vent and the candy would melt. Sometimes, we'd hunt for eggs and miss a few. Find them by smell a few months later. We ATE eggs that were in our baskets. Once, I opened one of the hard boiled eggs and inside, it was desiccated—like almost entirely disappeared. I thought, well, I probably shouldn't eat this one. It was left up to me to decide when an egg was too rotten to eat and when it was just fine. I have no idea of how many not just-fine-because-they-didn't kill-you eggs I ate."

"What you don't know may, or may not, kill you."

"Well, the other egg story is about 4-H."

"I didn't know you were in 4-H."

"I was. Our teacher, Mrs. Holger, taught us to crack the eggs not into the bowl you're cooking with but into a separate bowl. I did it for years although nowadays I crack them right in. But she was insistent."

"Why? So you don't get shells in the stuff you're making?"

"No. So you don't get a bloody egg. She showed us. She lucked out actually. The first egg she cracked was all blood inside. It looked apocalyptic in there. Bloody bloody egg."

"Then, the next one she cracked—a mangled, chicken like thing. So disgusting and distorted."

"We never get those anymore from the store. Not a rooster in sight to fertilize the egg, I guess."

"Yeah. What about farms? But still. You know eggs—always associated with life and potential. But these eggs. Life destroyed. Thwarted potential."

"Yep. That's what my book is about." I told Bek, "Eggs are earth's artwork—some of it's dark and full of death and some of it's weird but oh my god, everyone has an egg story. Probably because something, like art, or stories, or dinner, comes from it."

I put this story here like Anne put her mother's recipe in a cookbook, like Tanya's father scratched on shells, like Okim, like Hui Lang speaks of her mother. Maybe by collecting these stories, we remember how we share them. The sayings about eggs are sayings for all. It's like hitting an egg with a rock. Eggs in a basket. So many eggshells you have to walk carefully. jī fēi dàn dǎ. You have to break so many to make an omelet. She's a good egg. We translate these saying across oceans. If you're looking for something to take with you as you move from home to home, or friend to friend, something that connects you beyond space and time, take an egg to sustain you.

Mohawk

It took four eggs whites, whipped in the bathroom and fingered into your hair, to get it to stand straight up. You could let the edges flop over the shaven sides of your head and look like a choirboy, or maybe more like a mop. In chemistry class, you sat not in the front but not in the back either. You loved balancing equations. Stoichiometry helped you sleep at night: this many carbons on this side, this many carbons on that. Thinking about the Periodic Table made it possible to stop thinking about the girl you kissed, really, too hard that night at the Massacre Guys show. Her mouth around the spigot at the water fountain. She wore a blue flannel and blue pants. She was everything the guys at the show were not. She wore no leather. She had no shaved parts. Her ears devoid of even a safety pin. She was either a total poser or a complete nonposer. It didn't matter anyway because her lips opened around that question mark of water and the way she answered it. Well, you had to take her sentence. She should be lucky you didn't take more, girl at a show at the Indian Center wearing no eggs for protection at all.

So many eggs, one small basket

Reddit is a social-news networking site, sorted by threads of topics. There is a Reddit site called "Weird Eggs" because God or someone loves me and wants me to have whatever I want, which is, at the moment, images of weird eggs. There are celebrations inside this sub-Reddit. From "rapping eggs" to "quadruple eggs" to "my hen is laying ginormous eggs," there is an egg festival going on inside the Internet. There are pictures of four yolks supported by one white called "quads" and images of super-tiny eggs the Reddit folks call "the tinies."

Reddit itself, like all clicking tools of the Web, is a kind of an egg. You can go deeper and deeper into sub-Reddit after sub-Reddit. The click breaks the shell. Cracked and opened, the new page reveals the innards—the matryoshka dolls of the reading world. Fertile links. Lines as blue as on a pregnancy test.

At a party at Maggie's house, I don't throw up but I collapse in the bathroom. I don't have a headache but the room is spinning. I am not drunk. I was recently upright and now I am downright. The ceiling is not my own, which makes lying down on the ground even lonelier. I do not feel like asking for help. I feel like standing up but my legs are jelly-like; they shake like whites of an egg hardening in a frying pan.

I manage to stand up and walk out of the bathroom, as long as my hands can use the walls for support. This is my friend's house so I feel badly about touching her newly painted walls and leaving my headprint on her floor mat and looking at her ceiling that is her private-to-pass-out-and-gaze-upon ceiling. I have overstepped my boundaries and should get out of there.

My friend Julie notices that I'm wobblier than usual, drives me home. She calls her sister who is a nurse. Her sister comes to my house. She asks if I want to go to the emergency room. No one wants to go to the emergency room. My side hurts, I tell her. She pokes. It hurts worse.

"Are you pregnant?"

I could be. I always "could be" pregnant. I am the Schrödinger's Cat of pregnancy. For two weeks following any period, I am definitely not pregnant. For the two weeks before, I am. Then my period happens. My period is the observer looking inside the box, killing the cat. Most of the time, I'm glad the cat is dead. Sometimes, the cat is alive. That is not always as good news for the cat as you might think.

Which came first: the box or the cat? The shell or the yolk? The yolk is not a baby chicken. It's a nourishment-providing sac like the placenta. The white is not a chick either. The white is like the amniotic fluid in which a baby chick swims. If the egg is not fertilized, there is no baby chicken. Just albumen (white) and yolk and if you're lucky, perfectly poached.

I went to the clinic the next day. They sent me emergency-like to radiology. Pain near your ovary that makes you pass out is the kind of pain that makes people think "ectopic." Ectopic pregnancies are dead cats and might predict dead cats forever if your fallopian tube explodes and only that one ovary produces anything at all.

My then-boyfriend-now-husband, Erik, came with me, wearing his JanSport backpack, which made me feel too young to have a baby, even an ectopic one. I wouldn't look at him because I was nervous and shutting down emotionally, which I do when my ovaries are involved and which might have been a sign for him to cut his losses and break up with me immediately—but he stuck around then, through the imaging, and is still here now. He gives me the benefit of the doubt that I'm hard shell on the outside and soft albumen on the inside. I could be fully cooked through, though. Neither of us is sure.

It turns out I'm not pregnant. I'm diagnosed with ovarian cysts. Cysts on your ovaries are very complicated because an egg is, essentially, a cyst. "A follicle is the normal fluid-filled sac that contains an egg. Follicular cysts form when the follicle grows larger than normal during the menstrual cycle and does not open to release the egg." The fluid-filled sac, that is not a fertilizable egg, sticks to your follicle and grows enough to hurt. I might have that kind of cyst or a might have a corpus luteum cyst. "The corpus luteum is an area of tissue within the ovary that occurs after an egg has been released from a follicle. If a pregnancy doesn't occur, the corpus luteum usually breaks down and disappears. It may, however, fill with fluid or blood and persist as a cyst on the ovary. Usually, this cyst is found on only one side, produces no symptoms and resolves spontaneously like an ingrown hair."[1]

The cyst, full of blood or fluid instead of a sperm or a baby, hurts with its imposter filling. The shell can't tell what is on the inside. It expands as it has been determined to do. It doesn't drop correctly, hanging on to the edge of the ovary, like a baby chick clings to its mother. These metaphors are painful, too. Clipping on the edge of something but never quite completing their task. An ovary produces a cyst that is like an egg but incomplete. But an egg, incomplete and unfertilized, is also only an unfertilized egg. The egg is as like a cyst as anything can be—a cyst is a copy of an egg but an egg is merely a cyst, properly clipped from its follicular host. The cyst, clinging by some stringy umbilicus, tugs on the follicle. Which is it that won't let go?

A woman is born with all the eggs she will ever have. All in one basket—or two, since she has two ovaries. The ovaries are like pulls on a pinball game. As the years go on, each ovary drops an egg, like sands within the hourglass. One down. Two down. Three down. Every baby you never had clicks down through the slot like bubble gum in a slot machine or Pez in a Pez dispenser or maybe skeet balls in a skeet shooter. Or BBs in a BB gun. Choose your metaphor based on how many kids you already have or want or don't want right now at all. Each egg pops out with its potential energy threaded around its DNA. The egg, already half human, shoots its way toward fertilization. The egg is also already on its way to menstruation; half yolk, whipped until frothy, tumbles down the fallopian tube. There are two million eggs already formed inside her. We knew we had a population problem. But she was born this way. You can't blame her. In effect, her mother, pregnant with her, housed her own two million eggs minus the one egg that has become the fetus that is the daughter who also houses her own two million eggs. Women are giant matryoshka dolls with these eggs that are sometimes cysts, sometimes menstrual fluid, sometimes babies.

When I wanted to have kids, I couldn't get pregnant. Schrödinger's point is well taken. Maybe that cat really is dead. I cursed myself for looking in that box. I cursed myself when I saw smeared blood on my underwear or when I felt that ordinary tug on my ovary that meant the albumen was disintegrating, the yolk dissolving. I started to diagnose myself. Maybe I had grown a cyst with hair and teeth, permanently residing in my body—an egg that was a hairball of a baby that the damn cat couldn't cough up. I feared I had polycystic ovarian syndrome, which means you have multiple cysts on each ovary, the most common cause of infertility in women. I don't know why I thought I could diagnose myself. I can't even pick one metaphor. You would think more would be better but in the case of eggs and kittens, one is really the better number.

Mining the female body for usable eggs is like mining the word "matryoshka" for possible anagrams, or at least words you can make from the letters in "matryoshka." These are like metaphors. Ham. Tank. Smoky. Tram. Task. All words that transfer us to the mother's mother insinuated then pulled back out again, anagrams as a kind of generational mirror.

Clichés are metaphors that worked so well that everyone liked them, just like babies. Metaphors full of possibilities, of perhapses and maybes, are like those cysts attached to the follicle—multitudinous, unfinished, and yet, still fully present. Potential energy sapped that can't quite become kinetic. Either way, metaphors reproduce similarities but not exact replicas. Two million eggs don't turn into an exact copy of the mother. The chicken that laid an egg with four yolks today lays an egg with only one tomorrow. The metaphors fertilize and mutate. And like the two million eggs you may fertilize or you may flush, another one will come along.

But metaphors can be hopeful, even healing. Inside the Reddit, someone posted a picture of an egg that cracked inside the chicken then healed before the hen laid the egg. Even many cracks can heal. Eventually I got pregnant, although for all I know there are still cysts growing every which way off my ovaries, decorating my follicular tree with fluid-filled ornaments. Inside those cysts is another cyst; inside that one, another. The metaphors don't stop just like the stars don't stop or the babies don't stop or the eggs don't stop and the Reddit threads don't stop. The sheer abundance of the universe should remind you that Schrödinger had many boxes and many cats. A cat is always alive somewhere. An overly curious person cracks the egg to find out.

Which came first? Chicken porn can help you make up your mind about eggs

I pretend I'm considering milk—soy, organic, local, cheap, rBst-filled, but really I'm checking out the egg-shoppers. There are as many choices for eggs as there are for milk—white, brown, large, extra-large, grade A, organic, cage-free. Most people open the refrigerator doors and pull from the third shelf automatically. It's easier to reach and the third shelf is where all the caged-hen eggs have been housed for decades. Who wants to think every week about which kinds of eggs?

Studies show that too much choice can paralyze decision-making, which is what I'm emulating as I stand in front of the milk section. The *New York Times* reported on a study by Sheena Iyenger, professor of business at Columbia University. She discovered that although people say that they like the idea of choice, when push comes to shove the fewer the choices, the more likely you are to make a decision.

In the study, Professor Iyenger and her students set up sample tables in a gourmet shop in California. For the first 3 hours, they offered twenty-four kinds of jam; for the next few hours, they offered only six. "Sixty percent of customers were drawn to the large assortment, while only 40 percent stopped by the small one. But 30 percent of the people who had sampled from the small assortment decided to buy jam, while only 3 percent of those confronted with the two dozen jams purchased a jar."[1]

I'm trying to imagine twenty-four kinds of jam. I can get to six pretty easily: grape, strawberry, raspberry, apricot, peach. That's only five. After that, they get pretty speculative and hybrid. Chipotle-raspberry. Smoked peach. Black pepper-strawberry. It's fun to imagine each of those flavors on toast, if I had the time. But would my kids like chipotle-raspberry? Would I like something a little spicier? Apricot-habanero? The sensory experience of just imagining twenty-four jams is pretty intense. Maybe it's not too many choices but too many half-choices. Maybe the hard part is the hyphen. Where's my straight-up chipotle jam?

But in front of the milk, I am not paralyzed—at least not this time. Fry's milk is on sale for $1.99 a gallon and there is no rBst in their milk. I avoid hormone-filled milk because I don't want my daughter to grow breasts at age eight, but I admit that I have read only so much about the problems of milk and the pain of cows. When driving through Utah and Arizona, or any state in the west, really, I refuse to look the free-range (but still destined for some kind of cage) cows in the eyes. Like too many options, too much information can be paralyzing.

I've read too much about eggs, too much to save the buck fifty—the difference in price between cage-free and caged-in. For a dollar fifty, the hens that lay the eggs outside of cages get to walk around a little. They don't have their beaks cut off. They don't attack their cage mates with their beaks if they aren't confined to a cage. They get to pretend to be real chickens, although by "real" I'm not sure what that means. Cage-free, I guess. There are still fences and probably some cage time and I'm not going to spend three more dollars on a dozen eggs for organic feed so these chickens might be eating some of their old friends but I like to walk around, at least sometimes, so I suspect chickens do too, although perhaps they too are saddled with choice now that they're free to walk about. Should I meander over here? Should I eat this spider over there? Is that feed or manure? Do I call my own poop manure? I guess if it's used to fertilize my feed, which they are growing in that meadow over there. Does this make me a cannibal? Should I go look at the meadow? Is a meadow a crop if they feed it to me? Should I eat meadow or corn? Corn was a meadow once too. At least free-range chickens aren't confronted with the problem of twenty-four kinds of jam.

I read *The Handmaid's Tale* in eighth grade. I was shy and full of utopian dreams—so I read a lot about dystopian worlds. I remember the phrase "freedom from choice" as the mantra the government used to explain why the last fertile women on the planet should accept the roles of child bearers and bear children for the infertile, wealthy women. The way Margaret Atwood described the physicality of the fertilization scene was half industrial how-to manual, half porn. The fertile woman, if I recall, lay face-up on the top of the wealthy wife, who also lay face-up. Her head leaned to the side of the woman's stomach? Her breasts? So the man could pretend he was making love to his wife while he penetrated the fertile baby-maker. Caged between pretend wife and pretend husband, she bore the child that she had to pretend was not her own.

"Freedom from choice" isn't exactly what we're looking for. I think we're looking for easier ways to make decisions between choices. It's easy for me to choose cage-free. I have an extra buck fifty to spend on eggs. In California, caged-hen eggs are illegal. It's easy for Californians, then, to make the right choice. Perhaps if we called the eggs "eggs born of hens free from cages" instead of cage-free, the image of the hen trapped in a cage with four other chickens, their chicken breasts bulging against each other's like Sumo wrestlers, would become vivid in customers' minds. Perhaps then more people, at least more women who are likely to be sympathetic to the cagedness of other women, would choose caged-hen-free eggs. A cage-free egg doesn't really arouse empathy. We are accustomed to eggs in cages. Eggs are always caged inside cartons, inside refrigerators, on a third shelf where it has become natural to open a door and reach inside and choose a dozen. Maybe to disrupt the automatic caged-egg purchase, we need a chicken walking around the milk and egg section of the grocery store, bodily and mobile—reminding us that hanging around in the aisles, pecking at the options, limits those options by illuminating with fluorescent light the chicken's walking, choosy flesh.

Breaking a few eggs

There is a reason eggs come in dozens. I've brought eggs home with one precracked. I've dropped a whole carton on the floor and broke ten of the twelve. I've tried to poach an egg and punctured the yolk. Eggs, even cage-free, are pretty cheap. Words are pretty cheap too. Idiom after idiom, story after story, egg after egg, if one doesn't work, try another.

Such fecundity! Eggs the prime symbol of fertility. Mamas make eggs to make babies and mamas make eggs to make breakfast. I am grateful the planet is full of eggs and egg stories but, as long as it took to get the egg to become the kid, the kid brought the better story.

The human/egg interaction is an old one; human benefits from the egg more than the egg benefits from the human. Eggs for food and eggshells for art and egg ideas for metaphors about potential and thwarted potential. Eggs for religions like the Orthodox and Eastern Catholic Churches, Easter eggs are dyed red to represent the blood of Christ shed on the Cross, and the hard shell of the egg symbolized the sealed tomb of Christ—the cracking of which symbolized his resurrection from the dead—or in secular homes where we dye Easter eggs with PAAS egg dye and vinegar and hide two dozen fifteen times, because we best know we are alive when we are anticipating finding something that someone who loves us will make sure that we find. All of these are examples of the beautiful use of humans and their eggs.

But sometimes eggs are on the butt end of the human/egg interaction. For example, what we did to the eggs of bald eagles and other predatory birds by snuffing out mosquitoes. It took a while for Rachel Carson's *Silent Spring* to make its way into the worrying minds of mothers who not only loved bald eagles but recognized that the same poison that washes into the shell of a bird's egg washes into the thin skin of a human baby.

Then, the DDT went away, at least in large-scale application. The bald eagle began to recover.

There's a recipe to balance in the human/egg interaction—a little like balancing an egg on its bottom. Perhaps a little like balancing an egg on its bottom at the top of a very long needle. There's a pretty good chance the whole thing is going to tumble and fall, crack like Humpty Dumpty, but I've seen magicians before. It takes a steady hand and suspension of disbelief, but eventually the magician finds a sweet spot.

Humans create a lot of stuff: babies, soufflés, art, books, omelets, dances, cakes, music, 100-year eggs, factories, computers, shirred eggs, lithium batteries, scrambled eggs, cars, custard, plutonium, trichloroethylene (a cancer-causing industrial solvent), pâte choux, Herceptin (a cancer-defeating medication), frittatas, Roundup, poached eggs, hybrids of plum and apricot (pluot), hard-boiled eggs, DDT. In so creating, they sometimes destroy everything in their path. But then they build on that path again. Humans are possibly better revisers than writers of original material. Bring the DDT into the world. Delete the eagles. Delete the DDT. Put the eagles back in. A little like gluing a broken egg back together. A little shellac. A little egg dye and who will notice the difference?

It's Easter. Eggs are cheap. Of course, I don't buy the cheap, caged ones because I'm afraid of bad chicken karma. I'm afraid of cages. I surmise chickens are too.

I take an egg from the carton with the picture of the happy, cage-free cover on its top. I take a Sharpie.

On the first, I write other things I'm afraid of:

- People thinking I'm an idiot.

On the next:

- Kids won't adapt to world.
- World won't adapt to my kids.
- The lilacs will not bloom.
- The lilacs will bloom but too early.
- Not seeing a mountain lion.
- Seeing a mountain lion.
- Eating meat.
- KFC went out of business.
- Cleo the dog is dying.
- That Cleo the dog is taking a long time to die.
- That I will die one day.

I take each egg. I should crush it. Break it. Move on. Let it go. A life full of fear is no life at all. But I'm also deeply afraid of waste. So I crack each egg carefully, drop each one into a bowl. This is going to be a big omelet.

Blue planet, blue omelet

I wonder: If we run out of chicken eggs, can you eat a robin's egg? If the climate changes fast enough and devastatingly enough and no more eggs are forthcoming from the grocery store, can we eat every egg we run into?

Before the end of the world predicts the end of the Internet, I decide I should find out.

Instead of getting a direct answer, I find a Web site dedicated to how to treat an egg that is no longer in the nest. Kindness abounds, even on the Internet. The urge to repair and revise seems native to our species.

A mother asks the editors of the Journey North's Web site about a robin's egg lying naked and de-nested that her daughter found in her backyard. Can we put it back in the nest? Should we bring it inside and try to raise it in an incubator? The editors answer: "We know how much you want to save the bird," the Web site offers, "but that baby in that egg is most likely already dead. Either the parents abandoned it because it wasn't fertilized or a predator stole it from the nest. If the predator stole it and dropped it, the shaken baby bird would have died." They feel badly, the Web site, that they have to tell the young girl the truth, but, they caution, "it's a lot better for the baby to pass away now than to be born, live off the nutrients the egg sac supplies for one or two days and then die because the parents have already abandoned it." The Web site calls the dead birds "babies." Whether to soften or increase the impact of what they're saying I can't say, but the Web site is concerned both about the feelings of its askers and the long-term well-being of the robins.

"I know how sad it is to see these beautiful eggs and how very tempting it is to want to save the tiny babies inside. But it's just as heartbreaking to watch the babies start out healthy, with their egg sac to provide some nutrition for a couple of days, and then wither and die at our hands."[1]

This Web site tries diplomatically to tell these people that their attempts to be kind, to help out with the robins' eggs, does not help robins in general. At some point, they have to be forceful: "If the female was killed, the eggs are doomed." And, "Rotten eggs are NO fun!" "You are going to be [in] for serious heartbreak."

The Web site tries to spare people's feelings, to protect the robins, to suggest that people should probably just get out of the way. The Web site succeeds in educating people, but they probably hurt a few feelings. The cliché "You've got to break a few eggs to make an omelet" must be a powerful force at the offices of the Journey North. As much as humans want to save the birds, other humans want to save humans and the birds from well-meaning but ultimately harmful humans. The Web site wants to save us from each other.

The scientist's ethic that humans should observe, not mess with, the world around them is a sound one. Nature should run nature's course. I always thought that was kind of bullshit. Humans have fucked up nature already. Shouldn't they do what they can to bring some fish to the ice-lost polar bears, or pick up an egg that seems to have fallen out of the nest? But now I guess I should realize, leave it to humans to bring the polar bear a salmon with mercury or some fatty lipid that polar bears can't digest, or to leech oils from fingers to permeate the thin blue of the robin's egg, destroying the chick anyway. Humans are bad at creating a better environment for themselves, let alone other creatures. Always thinking we know best. How is it best to let a robin be born just so it can sing its starvation song to its missing mother?

I finally found some responses to my question, "Is it OK to eat robin's eggs?" The first answer will be, "No. It only takes 12 to 14 days for a robin's egg to hatch so essentially, you'll be eating a robin embryo." But in good Internet fashion, someone emerges with a rebuttal. "Sure you can. *Balut* is a delicacy in the Philippines, look it up." And so you do. (Look it up, not eat. Yet.) You find that *balut* is a boiled developing duck egg. In Tagalog, *balut* means "wrapped"—haute cuisine cooked adobo style—you eat the albumen, embryo, shell and all. Nowhere on Wikipedia does it say "robin's egg." Now you're back to square one and you're wondering whether to go ahead and try to save the robin egg or just boil it in the green chili sauce you made yesterday from the last of the Hatch peppers. You remember Wiehong's feelings about eating unhatched, fertilized eggs: Disgusting. You doubt it would be good. And what do you mean by good, anyway? A strong heart? A heavenly body? A perfect shell? Or a delicious lunch?

I don't think I'd eat a robin's egg. Would I eat a robin? I have two new kittens. They're Maine Coons. They like to get wet in the shower. The boy one meows like he's in heat. The girl one is quiet but will dart outside the second you open the door. The boy cat meows to follow her. He's in a different kind of heat. The kind that wants wild. That wants dirt. That wants bugs. I let the cats outside but I feel bad in advance. The robin's egg is safe but the robin himself is not. He's a tease. The cat, hot for wild, presses his body into the grass. He's as flat as a rock. As tightly wound as a bow. As focused as the tip of that arrow.

My apology is just as targeted. I say I'm sorry to the robin. But then the apology becomes diffuse. Regret is a human's first word. It's why we revise and revise our story. For example, I thought my dad was allergic to cats so we had to continually give ours away. I never looked at the other side of the story, that he kept letting us bring home kittens because one day, the right cat would cure his allergies.

I revise my beliefs based on what I want. Based on what the cats themselves want. I should make the cats stay in but the sound they make: that low meow that sounds like prison. There are so many house cats in the world and fewer and fewer songbirds because of them, every year, and yet, like the chicken, I want the cats to be free as a bird, I suppose, hypocritically, at the expense of the bird.

Humpty Dumpty, revised

Hypocrisy, thy name is human. I will sacrifice one species for the happiness of another. I recognize the trouble with procreating. More kids means more plastic, carbon, paper, cows, pigs, pizza. I am a resource sink. But I promise, I tell myself, my kids will add more than they take. They'll balance out the carbon. They'll harness the energy from the sun. They will revise this bad shit their parents and their grandparents left behind. Like an erasure poem, they will delete the idiotic parts of their mother's memoir. They will leave the planet better than they got it. They will science the hell out of it. They'll make bald eagle eggs that can survive nuclear blasts. They will make soufflés that rise even when their own kids stomp on the kitchen floor.

"Eggshells grow like crystals," I tell Max. Max, who is five, wants to be a scientist—more specifically a geologist. He has a book we bought used called *Minerals and Rocks*. For two weeks, he wouldn't let it out of his hands, clutching it in his sleep at night. He took it to school. He brought home rocks from school. His backpack got heavier and heavier. He took the book hiking. Every seven feet, he stopped. Picked up a rock and tried to identify it. Flagstaff, where we live, is not, from what I can tell, very rock-diverse. Sandstone and volcanic rock. But he would check the color and heaviness, the crags and crevices, the lines and the edges.

"Is it granite?"

"I don't know. I don't think so."

"Is it metamorric?"

"Metamorphic. No. I think it's sedimentary."

"Sedentary?"

"No sedimentary. Same idea though. It turned into rock just by sitting there. It didn't have to go through volcanoes of fire like igneous or be crushed or burned like metamorphic."

"Sandstone is so boring. It just sits there," he says from the ground, wiping the dust out of his book.

"Let's actually start moving then. We don't want to be boring as sedimentary rock."

He stands up. I dust the sand off his butt. He puts his book back in his pack and starts forward. We make it another seven feet.

This half-mile hike takes 2 hours.

He takes the book to his grandma's. We have already done the experiment to make a fossil. Rub shells with Vaseline. Add some food coloring to some plaster of Paris. Tuck the shell on top. Make a new color of plaster of Paris. Add a slippery, Vaseliney shell. One more layer. One more shell. Let dry. You have constructed eons in your kitchen. But when we tried to separate the layers to see the fossil imprint, our quick dinosaur dig, we couldn't. Zoe, took the plaster outside and smashed it on the driveway. Finally, one layer broke open. Inside, the fossil imprint crenellated as a fan. The shell broke too. An inside-out egg, broken all the way. Also, it was Zoe's shell. She was kind of mad.

At his grandma's, he wanted to make a crystal. She was game. She had calcium carbonate (baking soda). She had two cups. She had a string. In the upstairs kids' bathroom, Max stirred the baking soda into each cup halfway filled with water, the string hanging between them. He and his grandma waited. Max stood at the counter.

"When is the crystal going to come?"

My mother-in-law consulted the book.

"In three to five days, the calcium will crawl up the string and the crystal will begin to form."

"Three to five days?!?"

Max might turn into a fossil before that.

He finally relents with the promise of a doughnut and a show. Maybe *Mickey Mouse* is on. Or *Teenage Mutant Ninja Turtles*.

Five days later, he returns. Around the string, a knot of rock has formed. Max is both amazed and bored. It looks like salt wrapped around a string.

"Can I eat it?"

"No. It's a rock."

"Salt is a rock."

"This is baking soda."

"Oh."

It is devious to unwind a kid from his straight-arrowed logic but if you don't, you'll be stuck in the bathroom, eating salt all day.

An eggshell grows the same way as a crystal, creating its external from its essential self. The wet sloppy egg mass sends mammillary protrusions out like a string. Around them, in the sea of amniotic fluids, particles of aragonite begin to pile. Calcite, a form of calcium carbonate, collects on top of the aragonite. Columns of calcite grow upward, connecting in midair, at the edge of egg shape, hard as a rock, as breakable as patience.

Do eggs bring skunks?

Sometimes, you don't have to worry about breaking things. Sometimes, the repair is in the breakage, like when you try to amend your own soil with your own compost to grow tomatoes. You can add eggshells to your compost. The nice thing about eggshells is that they're already broken. There is, or should be, little worry here. If you're adding them to your compost pile to boost the calcium carbonate content of your soil, well, there are quicker and easier ways. You'd need a lot of eggshells to change the calcium levels of your soil, but let's imagine that you mainly want to reduce your contributions to landfills. You like the idea of more dirt. You do, in fact, eat a lot of eggs. The smaller you make the pieces, the better. Sometimes you save the eggshells, put them in a plastic bag, and invite the kids to stomp them into oblivion. There's a recommendation online that, if you really want them to decompose and add chemical balance to your soil, you should grind them up in a coffee grinder. I thought the whole point of the compost pile was that I didn't have to do too much extra work. Saving them up to grind in big batches is as much work as I can manage. Finding an extra coffee grinder goes one step beyond.

But I do worry. Should I wash out the thin membrane that sticks to the shell? If I don't, will the raccoons invade the compost? Will the eggs invite skunks? Will skunks spray my dog? If I wash them out, am I wasting water? Would it be more efficient to toss them in the garbage? Usually, I crush them up in my hand. This is not recommended. The shells can cut through skin. That saying, good deeds punished. Not that I was being that good, crushing eggshells, saving them from the landfill but still, I did need a Band-Aid and now I worry about the kids crushing them with their feet. I make sure they're wearing shoes but sometimes my kids get tired of wearing shoes. It's becoming overwhelming now, having to worry about already-broken eggs.

As Journey North's Web site says about saving the robin's egg, saving the planet isn't going to work if it doesn't lead to long-term success. In human terms, that means easiness. People are horrible at denying themselves what they really want. If you want to drive your Hummer to the store and leave it idling in the parking lot, you will do so. If eggs are bad for me, I will eat them in secret. If eggs are good for me, I will flaunt my Cool Hand Luke skills. You will admire me or despise me, depending on the circumstances. I read somewhere that your happiness is inversely proportionate to how much you care what other people think. I might be the saddest person in the world. I just got a rejection from an internal university grants program. They did not like my font. They didn't think I answered the question about how significant my book about sustainability and suicide would be. They claimed that it was a well-known fact that looking at situations from different perspectives is a way to create empathy. The idea that I was rehearsing old ideas? Well, aren't we trying to be good recyclers? Maybe they would have preferred my egg book, instead?

🥚

At a birthday party I went to when I was eight, I made myself busy in the kitchen. I asked Mrs. Larkin if I could help her bring in the cake plates.

"No, Nicole. Go have fun. I think they're starting the games."

"Exactly. Please, may I help throw away some garbage?"

They're playing the spoon game—the one where you carry an egg across the lawn and tip it into your teammates spoon so they can turn and run the other way. This game is pointless. And wasteful. And I am very bad at games. Or, rather, I hate games because I hate to lose. I might win, but probably not and so why bother, especially with this egg that really could be put to better use in a quiche or a soufflé.

Still, I'm ten so Mrs. Larkin kicks me out of the kitchen to make me play. I try to find a team. The teams were evenly numbered without me. Now I'm just an extra complication to what should have been a straightforward game. The thirteenth egg.

An egg topples into my spoon. I walk slowly but the competition to my left is practically running. I pick up my pace but then the egg starts to wobble. You can't drop the egg. I want to hold it. Why can't I just put my finger on the top? I'd win then for sure. If I can't do dishes, then at least let me cheat.

I don't drop the egg but my team doesn't win. On to the next game. Someone pulls out a bandana. Pin the tail on the donkey is the worst. Everyone can see me. I can't see them. They are laughing as I walk away from the tree upon which the donkey is hung. I walk toward the grass. I turn sharply to my left. I knock an egg off the table. It cracks. I am nowhere near the donkey's ass.

Would you eat a red speckled egg?

A vulture's egg wears its turkey neck on the outside in speckled red dots, like a crime scene. You take the spattering as a sign of bloody lust. Its speckles seem arbitrary and disorganized, just like love or a body accidentally run over by a car. The turkey vultures circle over the dead squirrel. The best part first: entrails where old food doubles nutrient value. You can take home part of the entrails, carry them like a worm your brethren robin might take, to the baby chicks, if they have in fact broken out of their speckled egg.

The speckled eggs make a force field to protect against predators. No one wants to eat something that looks like it has the measles (or, at least humans do not, as long as they have access to perfectly white caged or uncaged eggs). You might not eat a blue robin's egg because blue is a rarely edible color. You've met robins face to face. You couldn't do it. They sing so cute.

Turkey vultures don't sing. They have nothing to say. They don't need to talk. They have each other. One, two, three vultures fly in like B-52s. Well, bombers, until they tighten their circle. Then they tilt into whirlpools spinning wind into spools. They can ride forever in a tornado of wings. Tilt wing right, there's a dead squirrel over there; a tilt of a wing to the left, a dead raccoon over there. A double wing tilt thanks the cars for their driving, their wheels for flattening, their steerers for not really noticing the tufts of squirrel brown rolling in front of cars. Lunch. Snack attack.

If I could smell blood from miles away, would I run toward or from? I can write the word "blood" all over the page but when I smell it, I don't gag but I don't salivate either. When it's my period and I forget to change my pad for a few hours, the smell of blood wafts up. It makes me think about old blood. Baby death. Old mothers. But vultures, they aren't repelled by death. Blood makes them feel alive. But they don't love it either. The vulture is a practical bird. They are the cleaner-uppers of death, the service industry workers. They do their jobs. They don't get rich off it.

Hardly anyone goes out of their way to violate a turkey vulture, mostly because they associate them with death. Death creates a good bubble around the vulture and its egg, although human industry trickles into their food sources, which is why vultures don't attend every death.

The incredible, edible egg

People who see the value only of the board-acre in the trees, the arty potential of a woman's thigh, of the calories of an egg, do not see the filaments of web, dust, and water vibrating between the pine needles, do not see the connections in the gray seams of the tree that run like veins on the egg of a shell. Trees do make two-by-fours. Women make fine objets d'art. Think of all the writing to describe the exact angle of the woman's jawline, the softness of her eyes as she gazes upon the man. Think of the eggs, cracked, shelled, blended with cheese, dotted with butter. Eggs are meant to be eaten. It's work to persuade those people to see differently. Sometimes, you have to trick them. Invite them over for eggs baked in ham cream, while they wait for the surface area of the cream to coat their tongue, read them your story. Sometimes it's hard for even me, supposedly trained to see the stringiness of the egg mess and imagine the well-formed quiche. Sometimes, I look at an egg whole in its shell and wonder at its weight. What am I to do with you? I ask myself. Are you coalescing or do you remain all string theory, resonating alone, although, I hope, still resonating.

What is a cloaca?

Perhaps instead of Taking Back the Night with a march, I can take back the egg with an experiment. I put an egg in my vagina. I was reading someone's essay about memory and weeds and about how you might never get what you want, so right now seemed the time to try it. Max was watching the PBS Kids show *Wild Kratts*—the one about frogs and how not to just to let your bullfrog escape into the wild because they will eat anything that fits in their mouths, and bullfrogs have big mouths. They can eat eggs whole. So can vaginas, I wonder?

The egg was cold. I was afraid to put it all the way in. But it fit perfectly. So perfectly, my vagina could swallow it up and hold it there forever. It would never turn into a chicken though. I kept my fingers on the narrow point. I was afraid if I put both ends in, I wouldn't be able to get it out. I was afraid that it would crack and messy egg yolk would slide down my leg. No worse than other mucousy remnants that slithered out of there but again, cold. And somewhat wasteful. The abortion police might be on my case for allowing this through-a-human-vagina decay and fall. Out of a chicken, OK. Out of me, well, I've got the Supreme Court on line one. There's always a vagina guardian.

The egg was still cold. I rinsed it off. I put it back in the carton. It's no grosser than a chicken's vent—in fact, less gross. Through a chicken's vent come all effluent, shit, piss, and eggs. My vagina is comparatively pure. Just egg after egg, sometimes baby, egg, then egg again. I put the egg back in the refrigerator. The USDA explains why you must refrigerate your eggs in the United States even though they do not in Europe. In the United States, egg producers wash the eggs, removing the cuticle, a thin coating on the outside of the egg that prevents other kinds of contamination. In the UK, the unwashed cuticle keeps microbes out. The most common microbial contaminants of the inedible or rotten eggs are the genera *Alcaligenes, Acinetobacter, Pseudomonas, Serratia, Cloacae, Hafnia, Citrobacter, Proteus,* and *Aeromonas.* Words from Ovid's *Metamorphoses.* A seed of an idea is a good thing; a seed of a bad microbe in your gut, not so much.

I find it funny what we consider dangerous, what we consider gross. By not washing their eggs in the UK, they're actually protecting against microorganisms. Dirtiness leads to better health. And not all microorganisms are bad anyway. In your stomach, good microorganisms keep in check bad organisms. They help you digest food, process toxins, dissolve fat. Some say that even eating your boogers can boost your immune system by introducing your body to surrounding pathogens. On CBS News's Web site, an article feature by Dr. Scott Napper, a Canadian biochemist, claims that "By consuming those pathogens caught within the mucus, could that be a way to teach your immune system about what it's surrounded with?" Napper said he asked his students, adding he's seen this behavior in his two daughters, who may be just "fulfilling what we're truly meant to do." Dr. Napper claims it's a sweet taste; I think it's a bit more savory, a little like eating a runny egg yolk. Vaginas are not gross. Boogers are not gross. Eggs are not gross.[1] Kristeva, eat your heart out.

What seems less gross but is actually grosser is a stomach devoid of microbes, a soil devoid of microbes, a forest devoid of microbes. As we pesticize and sanitize and neutralize the environment around us, we have fewer and fewer checks and balances. "Half of the world's human population is infected with the stomach bacteria called *Helicobacter pylori*, yet it causes disease in only about 10 percent of those infected. Other bacteria living in the stomach may be a key factor in whether or not *H. pylori* causes disease, according to a new study led by scientists at the University of California, Santa Cruz."[2]

The egg has several layers of defense from infiltration. The outer membrane, although we spray it off in the United States, keeps eggs fresh even on the counter in Europe. The shell itself acts as cuticle, keeping the bigger, aggressive infiltrators out. The inner membrane, the one, if you recall, that let the tiny water molecules out but not the big sugar molecules in, provides another layer. But even so, sometimes salmonella makes it through. Did you know that your own body protects against salmonella? A little salmonella won't kill you. Dip your finger in the cookie batter. It's OK. It's just a whole lot of salmonella that your own body's bacteria can't fight: Beware the uncooked egg, but only in prodigious quantities.

Industrial farming and animal production has led to fewer and fewer species of food. Antibiotics used in industrial farming have decreased the number of good microorganisms combatting bad microorganisms. One bad microbe can destroy a food system based on monoculture, like what happened with the Irish Potato Famine and the potato blight. A more diverse food system, like a well-diversified 401K, hedges against disaster and the "dirtier" that food system is, the more well diversified with microorganisms, the more a defensive microorganism will take on an offensive one. Don't wash your eggs if you grow them at home, then you can leave them on the counter. Eat your boogers. Don't be afraid of vaginas. Keep this planet dirty, is the lesson of the microbes.

A million-year-old egg

A condor leaves her egg out all the time. Primarily because she wants to hatch it, not eat it. She takes her pretty, fat egg and beaks it around in a cave or behind rocks. These birds have survived in one shape or another since the Pleistocene. Without nests. By nudging their eggs behind rocks.

But leave it to humans to decimate the remaining dinosaurs. Habitat destruction (what else is new) plus lead bullets (condors eat carrion and carrion is often left behind by hunters, their bullets leeching lead into the ground and the gut of a passing condor) equal no more dinosaurs. Condors seem to be at the wrong end of the DDT food chain. The eagles have recovered but condor eggshells are still thin, thin, thin. The species is so well managed (if also so well destroyed) by humans that the humans take every condor egg from its not-too-hard-to-find hiding spot and place it in an incubator to thicken the shell, to give the condor a fighting chance.

One of the missions of the Grand Canyon Trust is to reduce the amount of lead condors consume. Working with Babbitt Ranches, the Trust carts freshly killed—by stun gun instead of leaded bullet—cows toward the Vermillion Cliffs near the borders of Arizona and Utah. They leave these dead, expensive carcasses out in the field for the condors to eat instead of animals shot by hunters, left for dead, bullets left behind to hamper egg growth. The condors eat the filets, the T-bones, the skirt steak. They eat the kidneys and the intestines. They devour the eyes and the tongue, cleaning up the decaying planet, now, with less lead and thicker eggshells.

I would like to design a big magnet that sucks up all the lead in the condors' territory. I'd like to organize a search group that searches for lead, step by step, like archeologists search for ancient burial grounds or search parties search for missing children. Step by step we'll cover the desert, our pockets heaving with spent shells, condors as big as small airplanes flying over us, tipping their wings at us, providing a little shade.

It is humans who do so much. And undo so much. A constant revising.

A lot of pressure on one egg

Once upon a time there was an egg full of a chicken. Before that, whatever laid that egg had not quite evolved to full chicken status. Thus, the egg came first. Evolution is where we tuck all our hope.

Perhaps my kids will undo what their parents and grandparents have done. Perhaps, once they've recovered from the lead poisoning we've leeched into their brains from the lead pipes and lead bullets and lead residue from turning uranium into plutonium, they will return the lead, PB on the periodical table, to its rightful place, deep in the ground where neither condor nor child can swallow.

Jeanette Winterson wrote this in one of her memoirs: "Into the clockwork universe the quantum child. Why doesn't every mother believe her child can change the world? The child can. This is the joke. Here we are still looking for a savior and hundreds are being born every second."

It's the height of hubris to expect this of my children, but I do expect it. Or at least hope.

Sidewalk cooking eggs

I bought a "solar oven" as a last-minute Christmas gift for my daughter or for my son who may or may not have had one gift more than the other. This oven was meant to be the gift equalizer and I gave it to one of them, the daughter or the son, at Christmas, six months ago now, so I'm not sure who was equalized. The solar oven cost $14.99 and was probably too expensive for a flat square of cardboard and a flat square of foil but today is the first day of summer, the kids had their last day of school last Friday and it is already 10:00 a.m., which in summer boredom terms means summer is already interminable and they are reaching for the one last Christmas gift that might stave off what I told them earlier, like at 9:17, that if they asked again what should we do that they would be sent to the Flagstaff Athletic Club summer camp which seems fun—baseball! volleyball! swimming!— but which is apparently the worst camp in town because the counselors are just recruits from local high schools and are paid, I assume, since this is the least expensive camp in town, not enough to fake having fun playing volleyball, or baseball, or go swimming with a bunch of 5-to-12-year-olds, and are, unlike other camp counselors in town, mean. Plus, according to my daughter's good friend, they make you change for swimming in front of everyone which is sweet if you are living in a utopian universe but for those of us raised by puritans and Americans and child molesters, it's awkward to be a nine-year-old boy and change in front of a bunch of nine-year-old girls. The threat of FAC camp is my only weapon. I've deployed it already once this weekend when they asked if we could go swimming again tomorrow.

"If you want to swim everyday, you can go to camp."

"Can we go swimming the day after tomorrow?" Zoe, the fully clothed ten-year-old, asks.

"Maybe."

"What about the day after the day after tomorrow?" asks the five-year-old.

"Remember the nice water bottles FAC gave you last year? Go find them," I threaten.

No one went to look for the water bottles but no one brought up swimming again. Instead, they pulled their "solar oven" from their closets (plural pronouns for my lack of awareness of which one pulled, or from whose closet). The cardboard folding system was not kid-friendly. Origami skills I do not possess. Still, we managed to insert tab A into slot B enough times to make a cardboard something resembling a box. With wings. Like a bird. More successfully, Max constructed the solar capturer—a foil Vishnu with arms opening out, invoking sun. Or maybe like the lunar module. We hooked the sun capturer to the oven capturer. Voila. Stove-like entity. The instructions gave us choices. We could use the adhesive tape that came with the contraption. Each piece of tape indicated, by changing color from yellow to pink, that the inside of the oven had reached 70 degrees. It was already 70 degrees outside. We could also insert an oven thermometer but I had made fried chicken the night before and not a thermometer in the house, I learned from my blackened chicken, reflected the accurate temperature. The other two choices were to insert an egg or a piece of chocolate into the oven. The chocolate had already melted to the backseat of my car where my children are building a hut to live in when the apocalypse comes and they have no parents and they have to subsist on the remnants of goldfish crackers and Skittles. They will make another, better, solar oven from foil gum wrappers and leftover Dum Dum sticks and all the art they make every day in preschool and in fourth grade that we are saving for posterity or in the advent that we make it through the apocalypse or need new art after the apocalypse or need fire starter in the worst draft of the apocalypse.

So an egg was an obvious choice. It wasn't hot enough to cook an egg on the sidewalk but it was sunny enough to insert an egg into a solar oven to achieve "soft boiled" status. We put the egg in the solar oven. We taped the oven shut. We directed the foil sun capturer toward that unguarded and unaware sun. The egg never knew what hit it. The solar oven sucked up that sun. The temperature rose and rose. The egg in its shell shrunk from the heat.

Or at least we hoped that's what it was doing when the wind came up and tossed the solar oven across the yard. Zoe opened the oven. The egg was leaking. "Oh my god, ew," Zoe said. She does not like slimy eggs. Or leaking eggs. Or eggs really, at all.

I took the brown egg from her. "Oh man. You used a farmer's market egg. That's like fifty cents an egg."

"I thought that's all we had," she said.

"No. There are some other cage-free eggs. Those are only like twenty-five cents each. I'll get another one." Somehow, now that we were wasting eggs, throwing them across the yard for the vultures, I wished I had a dozen regular, caged-hen eggs. My science experiment buds seem to have no conscience at all. "Eggs on sale for $0.99? Let's see if gravity works," I think to myself.

I took the leaky egg in the house. I got her another egg.

"Let's put this one on the ground. And some rocks inside the box." It's Flagstaff. It's May. The wind gusts can hit 60 mph. I should tie the egg to the box, the box to the picnic table. But no one can leash an egg. And what's the point of an oven if a rock can't make it stick around?

We spent the next couple hours angling the sun collector toward the sun. By the time the sun shaded the back patio, the picnic table, and the solar oven, three hours had passed. That's how long the instructions said it would take the egg to bake.

We took the oven inside along with the egg. Zoe carried the egg carefully, having been fooled once by weight and weather, didn't plan to get fooled again. I wasn't worried. The egg felt hot.

"Crack it," I told Zoe.

She did.

It wouldn't open. I had visions of rock-hard yolk, a whiff of the thousand-year-old egg Chinese delicacy or a desiccated found-six-months-later Easter egg.

"Crack it harder."

She hit it hard.

It oozed out into her hands just like the first, nearly uncooked egg, possibly a little more slowly.

"On *Curious George*, they cook a whole lasagna with a solar oven." Max is disappointed in the fact I do not possess solar baking skills like the man with the yellow hat. Zoe is scrubbing the goo off her hands, shaking her head at me.

The instructions read, "Do Not Eat This Egg."

Oh please. What's a little slow-cooked egg?

I take what is salvageable, though, having lost already one egg to science, and put this one in a frying pan. I add a little butter and some salt and pepper. I turn on the gas stovetop, which ignites without need of origami folding skills. I hope the microorganisms in my gut are ready to balance this baby.

I worry that mine is going to be a brief apocalypse.

A science fair every year

As I mentioned, Zoe has chosen an egg-based science project for the science fair this year. I don't think I persuaded her just because all I do is breathe, eat, and dream of eggs, but maybe my thoughts permeate her brain. The skulls of children are thinner and more susceptible to adult impressions.

I'm a little short with Zoe when I ask her about the experiment. "What are you testing—the hardness of eggs? The molecular constitution of corn syrup? I am not doing this experiment. You guys need to get it together. I wash my hands of it."

"Zoe, I mean, I'll help you, I just don't want to be in charge of organizing everyone. I like science. I like eggs. I like you!" I am sorry but she won't hear it. She's like the membrane, rebuffing me. The water molecules pour out of her like tears but my apologies cannot penetrate this sad membrane.

Zoe feels my disappointment. She's sensitive. Sometimes I think too sensitive. I told Rebecca once on the phone, if we were perfect parents, our kids would end up really boring. When you go a little nuts on them, you're seeding their interesting future. You're making them tougher. Adding calcium and carbon to the exterior of their soft innards.

But making interesting children, tougher kids, doesn't feel so good in the moment. I apologize. I revise. But I know that I have cracked my daughter's perfect shell as surely as the ground has been cracked open for coal and the ice has been cracked open for carbon and the egg has been cracked open for breakfast.

I keep revising anyway. I try again. I pick her up, even though she's ten, even though she is only five inches shorter than me. I carry her to the sofa and I tell her I am sorry. I didn't understand how much it meant to her. I didn't hear how harsh I sounded. I didn't understand how much weight I put on her when I told her to do it herself.

I begin to make it up to her by boiling eggs. In the morning, she'll soak them in vinegar for 24 hours. The vinegar's acetic acid reacts with the calcium carbonate of the eggshell to produce carbon dioxide, calcium, and water, dissolving the hard shell. Bubbles of carbon dioxide will form. The membrane surrounding the egg remains intact but the hard shell has completely disappeared. You've seen this experiment before (How to Cook a Planet). The egg still feels spongy but whole, like a ball of silly putty or one of those stress balls. I resist the urge to squeeze. The magic of science! But this is not the experiment!

The experiment demonstrates osmosis. The next step is to soak one of the eggs in corn syrup, the other in water. The corn syrup's sugar molecules are too large to penetrate the membrane of the egg but the water molecules are not, forcing the egg to shrink. The water molecules abandon the egg in search of freedom or greener pastures or they have a sweet tooth and love the water. The egg soaked in water grows! The water molecules move inside the membrane, like liking like and all, and the water molecules marry and connect, enlarging the egg as they have enlarged themselves.

You have to break the egg, or at least dissolve the eggshell in vinegar, if you want to make something new. Preservation forever isn't going to happen. The baby chick breaks out. The chef makes a soufflé. The artist needs her paint to stick. But when I was boiling the eggs for Zoe's project, I boiled them for 5 minutes, let them sit in hot water for 20 minutes to make sure they were hard, pulled them into ice water for 5 minutes too and reboiled them to help loosen the shell from the white. A couple of them cracked. The eggs' insides expanded—water molecules, heated, attempt to escape even their rigid shell structure. But when I cooled them the second time, the shells restitched themselves together. I don't know if it's a perfect seal but if you look at those broken eggs, they look as perfect as the others. Cooling down is good for all kinds of revision: hotheaded mothers, and hurt-feelinged daughters and words written and unwritten and planets that would like to be, if not fully uncracked, at least cracked and then repaired.

The sex lives of fish

Just because fish don't comingle to reproduce doesn't mean they're not sexy—although I am not privy to the sexiness of fish. The woman fish deposits her eggs and the man fish swings by later to fertilize them. This doesn't sound very sexy. Nor does thinking of *Finding Nemo* and the way clownfish deposit their eggs next to the sea anemone as added protection from whatever hoovered up Nemo's nonsurviving brothers and sisters. Tuna, warm-blooded, streamlined, have to keep moving to keep their gills oxygenating, are the opposite of clownfish and lay their eggs in the open water. One hopes that a man fish that also swims one body length per second will swim by the pile of fish eggs and deposit his deposit upon her deposit, which also does not sound sexy but does sound geologic like the Grand Canyon. In the Grand Canyon, the condor lays her eggs also somewhat dangerously. Perhaps the nature of the egg is a dangerous one. Life must start out in difficulty for it to have any chance to survive itself at all.

The salmon spawns with the most tactility of all the spawners. She digs a hole with her tail—right next to the anemone. And they say fish don't use tools. This fish tools a hole for its would-be babies which is also not so sexy except for sand particulating though the river water like star dust going super nova. All those galaxy babies. Don't babies make you thirsty? The male salmon does the same as the rest of these oviparous fish, just happening by, dropping his sperm on top of the eggs without even the trouble of getting the woman fish's number. Perhaps the male fish is a fourteen-year-old boy and his main interest is to spread his semen wherever he goes, including the public bathroom at the movie theater but it's OK you don't know that's what he's doing in there and he's fast and discreet although possibly not so sexy.

There are fish, like rays and sharks, that give birth to live baby fish—that must involve some fishy, sexy business going on. Tails are tools and penises are tools and maybe the fish penis digs a hole in the riverbed of his baby-mama's uterus. These fish are ovoviviparous which means they cannot choose between chance and umbilicus. The yolk of an egg still feeds it. Still, in terms of protection, the inside-the-mother plan seems safest yet.

Even more mammal-like are the reef shark and the hammerhead shark that feed their babies like you and I do. They are viviparous and what they eat, their babies eat, including clownfish for which, in *Nemo*, they feel sorry but in real life they just say nothing because they are fish and they do not talk. You'd think since the viviparous fish are more like us that they would be the sexy ones but the hammerhead has a silly-looking face and the reef shark also is bad at buying his girlfriends drinks.

But think of the sexy that is pure water. The fish, not needing lubrication, can fertilize not stickily. They can get off on the sheer force of water. Humans need hot tub jets or bathtub spigots to accomplish the same thing. The fish, fast, aerodynamic, uses the water as its tool. It rubs the fleshy sides, tickles the unobtrusive genitalia, makes the word "genitalia" sing like a siren song. The jelly-like eggs, fluttering out from behind the woman fish like so many bubbles from the air filter on an aquarium, make you reach for them. We watch as we long but the fish, eyes on the sides of its head, doesn't long for touch. She is ecstasy all the time, moving forward in one long stream of sex. Thousands of eggs. Out of such abundance, can there be desire? The man fish swims along, sometimes hours later, drops his thousand seeds upon the thousand eggs. Maybe desire needn't be dictated by scarcity. Maybe the fish takes the long view. A thousand would-be fish babies make for so much potential—so much potential becomes, like water, full of sexy friction, nearly kinetic, rubs constantly in an ecstasy of medium. The fish swims in constant thrall.

"The present was an egg laid by the past that had the future inside its shell"—Zora Neale Hurston

As it is said of beauty, so it is said of the egg. Perhaps for both beauty and the egg it *is* what's on the inside that counts. How do you draw the line between art/beauty and nature/egg? Possibly with hunger. The egg is a portable snack for snakes and raccoons and humans, easy to swallow, easy to palm, although this is a kind of portability that neither the penguin nor the duck had in mind. The egg in the hand is a cross between art and sustenance, fancy and function. Ferran Adriá, formerly of the Spanish restaurant El Bulli, defines cooking as "putting the egg on a plate." Any manipulation moves the object from the dimension of nature to the discourse of art. The plate becomes a frame. The egg is now embellished. The visual portends the egg's potential. On the cusp of opening—the anticipation—is the art. For art, as for hunger, one is quite willing to destroy nature's perfection to get to the edible insides.

If it's what's on the inside, not the outside, that counts, then it's a wonder we don't think of intestines as beautiful. We turn away when we watch a zombie on *The Walking Dead* pull guts out of the newly bitten, stringing the entrails around their tongues like spaghetti. Some people pass out, naturally, at the mere sight of blood. For the benefit of their husbands, wives tuck their menstrual pads deeply in the wastebasket, under Kleenex and toilet paper rolls. Perhaps it is not what is on the inside that counts but what we make of the insides.

The egg, as object d'art, occupies three territories: constraint (in its eggshell), potential (in its wholeness), and utility (in its squishy interior). Maybe that is a kind of recipe for art/writing, although paradoxical in its prescription. You simultaneously ruin and unleash the potential by cracking the egg, by invoking the formal constraints of the shell and then breaking right through them. You use up all the potential energy in mucking with the yolk and the white while at the same time forging new energies (see soufflé) for the viewer/reader/eater.

Hieronymus Bosch's *Garden of Earthly Delights*[1] is a painting about eggs. Actually, ostensibly the painting is about heaven, earth, and hell. But eggs abound! A painting in which very few actual, ordinary eggs but egg-like entities—full of potential, fragility, and fertility—appear. A triptych, the first panel shows Eden. Here, all is intact. A fountain is as ovate as an egg. A fat turtle-penguin-platypus crawls from the primordial sea, the creature's slow pull up the shore in transition, on the precipice of evolution, on the verge of giving birth.[2] The mountains arch like eggshells. The house-y structures in the background provide nests for birds, beckoning in, not out. The crowns of the forest-orchard grow bulbous as eggs. Eve's belly is an egg on its side, cradled by white, eggy hips. Jesus, Adam, and Eve's ovate heads pointy at the top, wider at the bottom—eggs balanced by godly necks. These are eggs on the verge of being fully eggs. In this panel, nothing is revealed about the inside of the egg. The shell completely obscures. It may even be empty which then would make it not an egg because an egg, although perfect and Edenic, is full of potential. It doesn't contain any drama if it's empty. It becomes significant only when cracked.

There is a photo of my sister Paige kissing my cousin-in-law, Emily, on the couch. I sit next to them with an eye mask on my forehead. My actual eyes are wide open, not in surprise so much as in emphasis. See how everyone loves each other? It's one of the happiest photos because Paige and I often argue about small things, like when I complain about the slow way someone young and thin crossed the street and about her complaining that I put four ice cubes in her tea instead of five. We complain because, like poetry, we must mark every moment. This moment, her kissing my cousin on the couch, is marked by praise instead of complaint and so my eyebrows raise up to celebrate.

I want my friend the painter, Rebecca Campbell, who knows my sister and my cousin-in-law, to paint this painting but you cannot arrange the insides of the painting for the painter. She cannot access the undercurrents of crosswalk and ice cube that are inside me. The significance of the kiss would be only exterior shell.

The second panel of Bosch's triptych depicts earth in all its temporal fertility and perverted beauty. This is the egg as flesh. Humans make use of those eggs: They ride in egg-like carriages, float in egg-like boats. A man emerges from a blue egg so a wren can feed him a worm. Women lounge on blackberry and strawberry eggs. Whereas in the first panel there was one egg-stemmed fountain, now there are five egg-based fountains, created for the express pleasure of humans to bounce atop and dive from. Humans bend their backs in arcs as perfect as eggs. Under arches, humans kiss and press their snake-as-in-Eden bodies. This place looks a lot like Eden but more crowded, more fun, sexier, and more sinister. Birds—merely slashes of paint in the first panel—in the second perch large as humans. They eye the humans as they fall, tumble, frolic, stumble, caress, and lie in eggs. The eggs, cracked, are ground level: human domain. Humans take the potential from the first panel and convert it to kinetic functionality in the second. The eggs are useful. The eggs are beautiful. The birds are worried.

It's easier to depict animals and eggs than to depict humans because humans have the capacity, and the tendency, to tell you where you went wrong. The blue shock of the robin's egg—the robin won't complain. There is the old story of writing about a woman whose friend died of cancer. I wrote about the friend going to Mexico. The Mexican doctors placed a jar of bees on her chest. Who am I to say that bees cannot sting the cancer away? But worse, who am I to write about a woman whose friend died in Mexico, alone? I have never even been to Mexico. I go to safer territory in my writing here. Rebecca.[3] My mom. My sister. My cousin-in-law. My kids. I may crack the social contract by writing about them but like that image of the healed egg, they forgive me my representations and my misrepresentations. I do believe they know I'm trying to get it right. I'll revise it if they ask me to. I'm trying to keep the shell intact. If we go mucking about the insides, it gets messy in there. I try to distinguish who is accountable for the white, who for the yellow. On the outside, at some distance, an egg, cracked but relatively unbroken, is a thing like a marriage or a sisterhood.

Is the third panel a warning of what becomes after art? After you break the egg? Bosch paints fewer eggs in the third panel in the *Garden of Earthly Delights*. There's a human dropping through an hourglass, a mandolin crushing a person and a book, a pink would-be fountain, now drooping spindles instead of expelling light—a heart, still beating, but gone unused. The biggest egg-like creature is a woman-statue, cut in half, the bottom gone, the top a construction zone. A man climbs a ladder to do some drywall work. Another man stands at the bottom of the ladder. His easel tips. His eyes stare into the vast cavern where the vagina should be. Without a vagina, there can be no egg. This shell of a woman, curved and cusped, turns to look at art gone wrong. Bad mandolin. Bad painter. Bad carpenter. They cannot repair the shell and they cannot move inside. The eggshell, unoccupied, is a kind of hell.

Once upon a time, I lay upon a sterile table. This table was not a nest. It was not an egg. It was exclusive, not inclusive. The baby wanted out of me. I wanted off of the table. The body convulses symptomatically. This does not seem natural. The body shouldn't heave and bend this way. The hips do not spread wide enough. The vagina does not spread vast enough. And yet, even this formal structure, this seemingly too-small body, could not turn this natural act into art. I breathed and tried to visualize the turtleneck of my vagina slipping over the head of the big-headed baby. All I could think of was turtles and how they lay soft eggs peacefully in the sand and although the beach sands were eroding and although the hotel developers were still abuilding, the turtles kept crawling up the sand. Plop a soft egg there, a soft egg here. If only I could have transformed avian. An egg through a cloaca is an evolutionary wonder. The human female body is at the early part of evolution—the egg, a more perfect evolutionary specimen, falls painlessly free from the bird. As I shook and shattered on the sterile table, I realized I wasn't the mammal. I was surprised to find that my whole body was the egg.

A Fabergé egg is an egg on a pedestal. It's an egg as a carriage. It's an egg fountain. The Fabergé egg is what we really want from our egg: a surprise inside and an inside that continues forever. Like matryoshka dolls, the Fabergé egg reveals not potential but immortality. Unlike the matryoshka doll, the Fabergé is not a reiteration of the original. Each layer reveals a new surprise. More of everything. Constant revision. Who knows what's inside that egg? A popsicle. A gravy boat. A salamander. A pair of dice. A key. A key to another egg. An egg holds an everything.

I do not want my children to be exact replicas of myself. I do not want my writing to be an exact replica of my brain. The inside of the egg is not reducible to its outside. I am small and limited. I want my books and my kids to be expansive, like meringue. Put them in a whisking machine and watch them grow and grow. I am not sure what the mixing machine metaphor is in this case. I guess for the books your brain is the KitchenAid, dear reader. And for the kids. Ordinary life whips egg whites pretty well.

The story of the Fabergé egg is a matryoshka doll in itself, a repeated effort by a Czar, Alexander III, to please his wife. His son goes on to copy his father. On Easter Sunday, 1885, the Czar gave his wife, Maria, what looked to be a simple enamel egg. But when she opened the egg by its golden chicken-feet clasps, she found a golden yolk. She opened the golden yolk to find a golden hen. And inside the golden hen appeared a golden crown and a tiny ruby egg. Inside. Inside. Inside again. She never wanted it to end but there is only so small a surprise a Peter Carl Fabergé can make. The next year, Alexander had Peter make her another egg. And, after his father died, Nicholas the II continued the commissions for his wife and his now-widowed mother. Fifty Fabergé eggs were made for the family. Forty-two eggs survive. The golden crown and the tiny ruby egg from the first egg were lost. Perhaps their loss was the catalyst for the outpouring of more eggs. Loss leads to greediness. Scarcity leads to abundance. Ever more ornate eggs to fill the hole the loss of tiniest egg left behind.

In 1991 I smoked 400 Marlboro Lights. I saved the butts so Rebecca could make a train for a wedding dress. I saved eggshells for her as well. On a mannequin, Rebecca pressed hundreds of broken eggshells, making a bodice and skirt of a thousand weddings either of us could have attended but hadn't, yet. We had staved off Utah's destiny for each of us for another year. At the exhibit, the dress stood in the middle of the floor, lights focused on that dress. All the eggs we had broken. All the lung cells I had destroyed. I was going to say, it's not often you can make something beautiful out of so much destruction but that isn't true at all. Look at the broken eggs in the Bosch painting. Just like out of a wedding dress steps a naturally naked, weddingly beautiful woman.

Writing is best when I sit down and the words just come but that only happens when I've been strict with my purpose. Write about eggs. OK then. Write a sonnet. Yes. Write about potential energy and Hieronymus Bosch. My students use the word "flow" to describe the kind of writing they like but I don't know if "flow" is exactly the same as the words just coming to you. Hard transitions can amount to a strong and meaningful flow but there are strings of unformed writings that flow into stringy nothings. The egg, cracked, innards flowing out into a bowl, is just a raw egg in a bowl. No one likes the stringy, unformed texture of raw egg. Scrambling provides some structure. Whipping the whites provides some form. Baking in ramekins with cream provides some constraint. Separating the eggs, whipping the whites and beating the yolks, adding béchamel and cheese, putting into the oven and waiting for it to soufflé provides some structure. Is adding asterisks the equivalent of structure? What if you turn the asterisks into egg emojis? Every section opens into a new, eggier section. There is a reason culinary school costs more than creative writing school. I can show you how to make a perfect soufflé over and over again. Repeatable results deserve exorbitant tuition.

If Bosch is mostly cracking his metaphorical eggshell against the hard form of the Bible and Fabergé is all potential, potential, ad infinitum, what do contemporary artists do with the egg? In Lucian Freud's *Naked Girl with Egg*, the naked girl, her body abundant, her stomach abundant, so much postholocaust flesh, these bodies so edible and abundant. The girl's aureoles, round and upward turning, mirror the two upward-facing fried eggs that lie next to her on the bed stand. The woman, her eyes whited out as the egg whites, has sustenance available but she does not seem to want or need it. One hand under her breast. One on her cheek. She side-eyes the egg. She is not hungry. She has sadness to fulfill her. She has exhaustion. Freud and his abundantly painted women with breasts sliding, men with penises flaccid: They are not procreative; they are not recreative. They are supine and spent. A whole human race tired of getting it together, tired of sustaining itself, tired of eating eggs. I long for the crush and emptiness of Bosch's hellish shells. At least everyone is hungry in apocalyptic hell.

The Romantics loved daffodils, egg-yolk yellow and full of promise. The world was an objective correlative. Think of Wordsworth's happy daffodils, how Wordsworth wanders "happy as a cloud." All that happiness signified by nature. Think of how he wants to bring the daffodils home and recollect them in tranquillity. He imagines daffodils and magically, he is transported to happiness. He has brought the daffodils into his mind, secured them there, and now uses them as a tool to propel him from his occasional outcast state. He brought the daffodils into his home like a hard-boiled egg, perfectly portable, sustenance for the soul. But our world is not Wordsworth's. The daffodils are blooming in February, in January in some places. The daffodil doesn't signal nature secured. It signals nature, unstable and changing, not captive to our minds.

Perhaps this is why the eggs in Freud's painting are cracked and cooked over-easy. The time for potential is over. The time for metaphor is over. We had better eat as many eggs as we can right now. Paint the moment as we see it. Eggs in metaphor and eggs in potential are time-dependent. We are post DDT, post Fukushima, post Greenland ice shelf. You can't count on the hardness or thickness of shell. You don't know if—in this hard-boiled thing when you crack it open—you will find a perfectly cooked and edible egg or an overcooked baby bird. Maybe this is why we write and paint on eggshells. We have a hard time with objective correlative. The egg, exterior shell painted, is still an egg. An egg, whole, means potential and possibility. Hard-boiled, portable, we can take it with us wherever we go. The insides might be the art we are looking for but we can see only with the hard crack of a scarce stone, courting the impossibility of repair.

Recipe for an already-cracked egg

This recipe is not USDA or FDA approved. No one will tell you to eat an egg that you found in a carton, cracked but not quite oozing. But if these are the end times, we need to be resourceful. We also don't have a lot of antibiotics running around so if we're going to cook this thing, we have to cook it fast and hard. If you're going to cook anything to death, you may as well do it by frying.

Egg for fried rice:

Crack the egg (a little more so the egg can indeed ooze out).

Beat the egg with a fork.

Unlike the slow and low scrambled egg recipe, turn your pan on super high heat. Add sesame oil. Heat it until nearly smoking. The very precipice of oil destruction promises also the destruction of whatever bad organisms slipped in between the crack, permeated the shell, migrated across membrane, infected the insides with seemingly endless versions of itself.

Pour in egg. Push the egg back toward the pan then cut across it, making a cross as you would to make an omelet. When the egg starts to stick to itself, let it set.

Flip it over. Cook it hard, again. Really, cook the hell out of it.

Slide it on to a cutting board. Chop it into pieces.

Cook carrots, garlic, ginger in vegetable oil. Add cooked rice. Season with soy sauce. Add peas. Return eggs to pan, cooking them one last time for good measure. Out of the death of so many bacteria, something like art transcends.

NOTES

The egg came first

1 http://www.bsu.edu/classes/magrath/205spring/le1/dogomyth.
   html: [Synopsized from Encyclopedia of Religion (New York:
   MacMillan,1987), vol. 4, pp. 393–95].

2 Bernard Doyle, "Creation myths." *Encyclopedia Mythica*. 2016.
   Encyclopedia Mythica Online. March 13, 2016, http://www.
   pantheon.org/articles/c/creation_myths.html.

3 David Adams Leeming, *Creation Myths of the World: Parts
   I-II Volume 1 of Creation Myths of the World: An Encyclopedia*,
   ABC-CLIO, 2010.

How to cook a planet

1 Harold McGee, *On Food and Cooking: The Science and Lore of
   The Kitchen*. Scribner 2004.

2 Antero Järvinen, "Global Warming and Egg Size of Birds,"
   Ecography 17, no. 1 (January to March, 1994): 108–10.

3 Stable URL: http://www.jstor.org/stable/3682938

4 John Platt, *Climate Change Will Scramble Polar Bears Diets and Eggs Aren't the Solution,* Earth Touch NewsNetwork April 1, 2015, http://www.earthtouchnews.com/conservation/human-impact/climate-change-will-scramble-polar-bears-diets-and-eggs-arent-the-solution.

All the eggs in Israel

1 Cara de Silva, *In Memory's Kitchen: A Legacy from the Women of Terezien*, translated by Bianca Steiner Brown (Northvale, NJ and London: Jason Aronson, Inc., 1996).

So many eggs, one small basket

1 Melissa Conrad Stöppler, Ovarian Cysts, MedicineNet 2/4/2015, http://www.medicinenet.com/ovarian_cysts/article.htm.

Which came first? Chicken porn can help you make up your mind about eggs

1 Alina Tugend, Two Many Choices, A Problem That Can Paralyze, *New York Times*, February 26, 2010, http://www.nytimes.com/2010/02/27/your-money/27shortcuts.html?_r=1.

Blue planet, blue omelet

1 http://www.learner.org/jnorth/tm/robin/facts_eggs.html

What is a cloaca?

1 Ryan Jaslow, *Eating Boogers May Boost Immune System,
   Scientists Say* CBS News May 21, 2015, http://www.cbsnews.
   com/news/eating-boogers-may-boost-immunity-scientist-
   suspects/.

2 Tim Stephens, *Bacteria May Protect Against Disease Caused
   by Stomach Infection.* University of California at Santa Cruz
   News Center. March 12, 2013, http://news.ucsc.edu/2013/03/
   stomach-microbes.html.

"The present was an egg laid by the past that had the future inside its shell"—Zora Neale Hurston

1 Laura Erickson, *Robin Eggs* Journey North: A Global Study of
   Wildlife Migration and Seasonal Change. 1997–2016, http://
   www.learner.org/jnorth/tm/robin/facts_eggs.html.

2 Paul R. Ehrlich, David S. Dobkin, and Darryl Wheye, *Eggs and Their Evolution* Stanford Birds. 1988, https://web.stanford.edu/group/stanfordbirds/text/essays/Eggs.html.

3 Reilly, Maura. *Taking the Measure of Sexism Facts and Figures*, Art News 5/26/15 3:45 p.m, http://www.artnews.com/2015/05/26/taking-the-measure-of-sexism-facts-figures-and-fixes/.

INDEX